BROTHER LAWRENCE

MY PRACTICE OF THE PRESENCE OF GOD

A Guided Devotional Journey Through the Complete Classic Text

with decorations by
LIUDMYLA STETSKOVYCH

SEA HARP PRESS

My Practice of the Presence of God — Brother Lawrence

This edition copyright © 2023—Sea Harp
An imprint of Nori Media Group
P.O. Box 310, Shippensburg, PA 17257-0310
"Be Much Occupied with Jesus"

Cover design and interior page design copyright 2023.

All rights reserved.

Cover design by Christian Rafetto

Cover artwork by Theodor van Merlen (II), after Abraham van Diepenbeeck, "Saint Augustine"

Foreword by Eugene Luning

All rights reserved. This book is protected by the copyright laws of the United States of America. This book may not be copied or reprinted for commercial gain or profit. The use of short quotations or occasional page copying for personal or group study is permitted and encouraged. Permission will be granted upon request.

This book and all other Sea Harp books are available at Christian bookstores and distributors worldwide.

For more information on foreign distributors, call 717-532-3040.

Reach us on the Internet: www.seaharp.com

ISBN 13 TP: 978-0-7684-7692-7

ISBN 13 eBook: 978-0-7684-7693-4

For Worldwide Distribution, Printed in the U.S.A.

1 2 3 4 5 6 7 8 / 27 26 25 24 23

Contents

Foreword...5

Introduction 7

Preface...9

First Conversation..13

Second Conversation 27

Third Conversation..51

Fourth Conversation..65

First Letter 95

Second Letter 107

Third Letter 131

Fourth Letter 137

Fifth Letter 151

Sixth Letter..159

Seventh Letter 167

Eighth Letter 177

Ninth Letter 183

Tenth Letter 193

Eleventh Letter 199

Twelfth Letter 209

Thirteenth Letter 217

Fourteenth Letter..225

Fifteenth Letter...231

About Brother Lawrence..................................239

About the Illustrator 240

Foreword

By Sea Harp Press

The Practice of the Presence of God is a short book with one central premise: That the human life is only LIFE when lived in "Life Himself" (1 John 1:1). Brother Lawrence, unwittingly, by simply having a series of conversations and writing a handful of letters, set out for posterity one of the greatest works of spiritual devotion ever. Yet, always, as its inescapable, throbbing heartbeat is that one aim of his daily life: Personal union with the God of love.

We at Sea Harp Press were struck in a recent reading how almost every sentence—certainly every paragraph—is worthy of a slow, studied pensiveness and meditation. Which gave us the idea for this "guided journal" edition: What if, in a day-by-day way, we slowly walked through the admonitions of Brother Lawrence and actually put into practice his style of "practicing the presence"? What if we truly took to heart the words that came from that man's earnest heart? What if we took our time with God in the very same way as he did? What if we *actively practiced* practicing the presence of God?

Thus, within, you'll find the unabridged conversations and letters from all previous editions, but, after each, you'll also find their contents broken into smaller, practicable portions. Each of these is given a single prompt—some are reflections, others actions, others prayers—that we have prayerfully put together for your use and enjoyment.

May this be a series of days rich with awareness of the ever-present God who so richly blessed the days of Brother Lawrence. We hope you finish these pages walking in vital union with Jesus, with His Heavenly Father, all by the present, indwelling power of the Holy Spirit.

Thank you for being part of the Sea Harp Family!

Introduction

By Hannah Whitall Smith

"But I fear, lest by any means, as the serpent beguiled Eve through his subtlety, so your minds should be corrupted from the simplicity that is in Christ."— 2 Cor. xi. 3.

THE VALUE OF THIS LITTLE BOOK is its extreme simplicity. The trouble with most of the religion of the day is its extreme complexity. "Brother Lawrence" was not troubled with any theological difficulties or doctrinal dilemmas. For him these did not exist. His one single aim was to bring about a conscious personal union between himself and God, and he took the shortest cut he could find to accomplish it. The result can best be described in his own words: "If I dare use the expression, I should choose to call this state the bosom of God, for the inexpressible sweetness which I taste and experience there."

What Brother Lawrence did all can do. No theological training nor any especial theological views are needed for the blessed "practice" he recommends. No gorgeous churches, nor stately cathedral, nor elaborate ritual, could either make or mar it. A kitchen and an altar were as one to him; and to pick up a straw from the ground was as grand a service as to preach to multitudes. "The time of business," said he, "does not with me differ from the time of prayer; and in the noise and clutter of my kitchen, while several persons are at the same time calling for different things, I possess God in as great tranquility as if I were upon my knees at the blessed sacrament."

This little book, therefore, seems to me one of the most helpful I know. It fits into the lives of all human beings, let them be rich or poor, learned or unlearned, wise or simple. The woman at her wash-tub, or the stone-breaker on the road, can carry on the "practice" here taught with as much ease and as much assurance of success as the priest at his altar or the missionary in his field of work.

All must feel that anything that brings the religion of Christ within reach of overworked and poverty-stricken humanity, in the midst of its ignorance and its helplessness, is a priceless boon, and this is what Brother Lawrence does. His "practice" requires neither time, nor talents, nor training. At any moment, in the midst of any occupation, under any circumstances, the soul that wants to know God can "practice the presence" and can come to the knowledge. The Lord of hosts is with us, the God of Jacob is our refuge, let the "seemings" be what they may; and we need but to recognize this as a continual, ever-present fact, and the inexpressible sweetness to which Brother Lawrence attained will become ours.

Hannah Whitall Smith

London, 1897

Preface

From the 1895 Revell Edition

THIS BOOK CONSISTS of notes of several conversations had with, and letters written by Nicholas Herman, of Lorraine, a lowly and unlearned man, who, after having been a footman and soldier, was admitted a Lay Brother among the barefooted Carmelites at Paris in 1666, and was afterwards known as "Brother Lawrence."

His conversion, which took place when he was about eighteen years old, was the result, under God, of the mere sight in midwinter, of a dry and leafless tree, and of the reflections it stirred respecting the change the coming spring would bring. From that time he grew eminently in the knowledge and love of God, endeavoring constantly to walk *"as in His presence."* No wilderness wanderings seem to have intervened between the Red Sea and the Jordan of his experience. A wholly consecrated man, he lived his Christian life through as a pilgrim—as a steward and not as an owner, and died at the age of eighty, leaving a name which has been as "ointment poured forth."

The "Conversations" are supposed to have been written by M. Beaufort, Grand Vicar to M. de Chalons, formerly Cardinal de Noailles, by whose recommendation the letters were first published.

The book has, within a short time, gone through repeated English and American editions, and has been a means of blessing to many souls. It contains very much of that wisdom which only lips the Lord has touched can express, and which only hearts He has made teachable can receive.

May this edition also be blessed by God, and redound to the praise of the glory of His grace.

CONVERSATIONS

First Conversation

THE FIRST TIME I saw *Brother Lawrence*, was upon the 3d of August, 1666. He told me that God had done him a singular favor, in his conversion at the age of eighteen.

That in the winter, seeing a tree stripped of its leaves, and considering that within a little time the leaves would be renewed and after that the flowers and fruit appear, he received a high view of the Providence and Power of God, which has never since been effaced from his soul. That this view had perfectly set him loose from the world, and kindled in him such a love for God, that he could not tell whether it had increased during the more than forty years he had lived since.

That he had been footman to M. Fieubert, the treasurer, and that he was a great awkward fellow who broke everything.

That he had desired to be received into a monastery, thinking that he would there be made to smart for his awkwardness and the faults he should commit, and so he should sacrifice to God his life, with its pleasures: but that God had disappointed him, he having met with nothing but satisfaction in that state.

That we should establish ourselves in a sense of God's Presence, by continually conversing with Him. That it was a shameful thing to quit His conversation, to think of trifles and fooleries.

That we should feed and nourish our souls with high notions of God; which would yield us great joy in being devoted to Him.

That we ought to *quicken*, i.e., *to enliven, our faith*. That it was lamentable we had so little; and that instead of taking *faith* for the rule of their conduct, men amused themselves with trivial devotions, which changed daily. That the way

of Faith was the spirit of the Church, and that it was sufficient to bring us to a high degree of perfection.

That we ought to give ourselves up to God, with regard both to things temporal and spiritual, and seek our satisfaction only in the fulfilling of His will, whether He lead us by suffering or by consolation, for all would be equal to a soul truly resigned. That there needed fidelity in those drynesses, or insensibilities and irksomenesses in prayer, by which God tries our love to Him; that *then* was the time for us to make good and effectual acts of resignation, whereof one alone would oftentimes very much promote our spiritual advancement.

That as for the miseries and sins he heard of daily in the world, he was so far from wondering at them, that, on the contrary, he was surprised that there were not more, considering the malice sinners were capable of; that for his part he prayed for them; but knowing that God could remedy the mischiefs they did when He pleased, he gave himself no farther trouble.

That to arrive at such resignation as God requires, we should watch attentively over all the passions which mingle as well in spiritual things as in those of a grosser nature; that God would give light concerning those passions to those who truly desire to serve Him. That if this was my design, viz., sincerely to serve God, I might come to him (Brother Lawrence) as often as I pleased, without any Fear of being troublesome; but if not, that I ought no more to visit him.

Today, write out and reflect on the story of your first encounter with God.

The first time I saw *Brother Lawrence*, was upon the 3d of August, 1666. He told me that God had done him a singular favor, in his conversion at the age of eighteen.

That in the winter, seeing a tree stripped of its leaves, and considering that within a little time the leaves would be renewed and after that the flowers and fruit appear, he received a high view of the Providence and Power of God, which has never since been effaced from his soul.

Today make a list of everything in Creation that reminds you of the "Providence and Power of God."

Meditate today on the time in your life when your love for God was most enkindled. Reflect on the circumstances, the setting, the practices of your devotion, the people with whom you were surrounded in that time.

Where does your employment presently have you? Who there needs to meet God? How are you ideally positioned to be their point of introduction?

That this view had perfectly set him loose from the world, and kindled in him such a love for God, that he could not tell whether it had increased during the more than forty years he had lived since.

That he had been footman to M. Fieubert, the treasurer, and that he was a great awkward fellow who broke everything.

That he had desired to be received into a monastery, thinking that he would there be made to smart for his awkwardness and the faults he should commit, and so he should sacrifice to God his life, with its pleasures: but that God had disappointed him, he having met with nothing but satisfaction in that state.

Ponder on the balance/imbalance between self-sacrifice and God-satisfaction in your life. Does He have something more or better for you?

God is presently present. Talk to Him today as if it were truly so.

That we should establish ourselves in a sense of God's Presence, by continually conversing with Him.

Make a list of the "trifles and fooleries" that distract you from the Presence. Which need to go?

_____
_____
_____
_____
_____
_____
_____
_____

That it was a shameful thing to quit His conversation, to think of trifles and fooleries.

What is the "highest notion" of God that you've most recently learned?

That we should feed and nourish our souls with high notions of God; which would yield us great joy in being devoted to Him.

What are the "devotions" which are most steadfast and fruitful in your spiritual journey? Make a list of everything devotional you've ever tried. Reflect on the "enlivening" qualities of each.

That we ought to quicken, i.e., to enliven, our faith. That it was lamentable we had so little; and that instead of taking faith for the rule of their conduct, men amused themselves with trivial devotions, which changed daily.

Draw a picture of what "the Church" means to your heart right now.

That the way of Faith was the spirit of the Church, and that it was sufficient to bring us to a high degree of perfection.

Think of practical, concrete ways you might surrender today's practicalities to the will of God. Then go and do so.

That we ought to give ourselves up to God, with regard both to things temporal and spiritual, and seek our satisfaction only in the fulfilling of His will, whether He lead us by suffering or by consolation, for all would be equal to a soul truly resigned.

How safe do you feel with the heart of God? Is He someone you can actively rely on?

That there needed fidelity in those dryness, or insensibilities and irksomenesses in prayer, by which God tries our love to Him; that *then* was the time for us to make good and effectual acts of resignation, whereof one alone would oftentimes very much promote our spiritual advancement.

Pray for the brokennesses of the world around you today. Be moved by the hurts you see.

That as for the miseries and sins he heard of daily in the world, he was so far from wondering at them, that, on the contrary, he was surprised that there were not more, considering the malice sinners were capable of; that for his part he prayed for them; but knowing that God could remedy the mischiefs they did when He pleased, he gave himself no farther trouble.

List the people in your life who have most taught you to follow God. For those still living, reach out and thank them. For those who are not, give thanks to God for them.

That to arrive at such resignation as God requires, we should watch attentively over all the passions which mingle as well in spiritual things as in those of a grosser nature; that God would give light concerning those passions to those who truly desire to serve Him. That if this was my design, viz., sincerely to serve God, I might come to him (Brother Lawrence) as often as I pleased, without any Fear of being troublesome; but if not, that I ought no more to visit him.

Second Conversation

THAT HE HAD ALWAYS been governed by love, without selfish views; and that having resolved to make the love of God the *end* of all his actions, he had found reasons to be well satisfied with his method. That he was pleased when he could take up a straw from the ground for the love of God, seeking Him only, and nothing else, not even His gifts.

That he had been long troubled in mind from a certain belief that he should be damned; that all the men in the world could not have persuaded him to the contrary; but that he had thus reasoned with himself about it: *I engaged in a religious life only for the love of* God, *and I have endeavored to act only for Him; whatever becomes of me, whether I be lost or saved, I will always continue to act purely for the love of God. I shall have this good at least, that till death I shall have done all that is in me to love Him.* That this trouble of mind had lasted four years; during which time he had suffered much. But that at last he had seen that this trouble arose from want of faith; and that since then he had passed his life in perfect liberty and continual joy. That he had placed his sins betwixt him and God, as it were, to tell Him that he did not deserve His favors, but that God still continued to bestow them in abundance.

That in order to form a habit of conversing with God continually, and referring all we do to Him, we must at first apply to Him with some diligence: but that after a little care we should find His love inwardly excite us to it without any difficulty.

That he expected after the pleasant days God had given him, he should have his turn of pain and suffering; but that he was not uneasy about it, knowing very well, that as he could do nothing of himself, God would not fail to give him the strength to bear it.

That when an occasion of practicing some virtue offered, he addressed himself to God, saying, Lord, *I cannot do this unless Thou enablest me*: and that then he received strength more than sufficient.

That when he had failed in his duty, he only confessed his fault, saying to God, *I shall never do otherwise, if You leave me to myself; it is You who must hinder my falling, and mend what is amiss*. That after this, he gave himself no further uneasiness about it.

That we ought to act with God in the greatest simplicity, speaking to Him frankly and plainly, and imploring His assistance in our affairs, just as they happen. That God never failed to grant it, as he had often experienced.

That he had been lately sent into Burgundy, to buy the provision of wine for the society, which was a very unwelcome task for him, because he had no turn for business, and because he was lame and could not go about the boat but by rolling himself over the casks. That however he gave himself no uneasiness about it, nor about the purchase of the wine. That he said to God, *It was His business he was about*, and that he afterwards found it very well performed. That he had been sent into Auvergne, the year before, upon the same account; that he could not tell how the matter passed, but that it proved very well.

So, likewise, in his business in the kitchen (to which he had naturally a great aversion), having accustomed himself to do everything there for the love of God, and with prayer, upon all occasions, for His grace to do his work well, he had found everything easy, during fifteen years that he had been employed there.

That he was very well pleased with the post he was now in; but that he was as ready to quit that as the former, since he was always pleasing himself in every condition, by doing little things for the love of God.

That with him the set times of prayer were not different from other times; that he retired to pray, according to the directions of his Superior, but that he did not want such retirement, nor ask for it, because his greatest business did not divert him from God.

That as he knew his obligation to love God in all things, and as he endeavored so to do, he had no need of a director to advise him, but that he needed much a Confessor to absolve him. That he was very sensible of his faults, but not discouraged by them; that he confessed them to God, but did not plead against Him to excuse them. When he had so done, he peaceably resumed his usual practice of love and adoration.

That in his trouble of mind, he had consulted nobody, but knowing only by the light of faith that God was present, he contented himself with directing all his actions to Him, *i.e.*, doing them with a desire to please Him, let what would come of it.

That useless thoughts spoil all: that the mischief began there; but that we ought to reject them, as soon as we perceived their impertinence to the matter in hand, or our salvation; and return to our communion with God.

That at the beginning he had often passed his time appointed for prayer, in rejecting wandering thoughts, and falling back into them. That he could never regulate his devotion by certain methods as some do. That nevertheless, at first he had *meditated* for some time, but afterwards that went off, in a manner he could give no account of.

That all bodily mortifications and other exercises are useless, except as they serve to arrive at the union with God by love; that he had well considered this, and found it the shortest way to go straight to Him by a continual exercise of love, and doing all things for His sake.

That we ought to make a great difference between the acts of the *understanding* and those of the *will*: that the first were comparatively of little value, and the others, all. That our only business was to love and delight ourselves in God.

That all possible kinds of mortification, if they were void of the love of God, could not efface a single sin. That we ought, without anxiety, to expect the pardon of our sins from the Blood of Jesus Christ, only endeavoring to love Him with all our hearts. That God seemed to have granted the greatest favors to the greatest sinners, as more signal monuments of His mercy.

That the greatest pains or pleasures of this world, were not to be compared with what he had experienced of both kinds in a spiritual state: so that he was careful for nothing and feared nothing, desiring only one thing of God, viz., that he might not offend Him.

That he had no scruples; for, said he, when I *fail* in my duty, I readily acknowledge it, saying, *I am used to do so: I shall never do otherwise, if I am left to myself*. I fail not, then I give God thanks, acknowledging the strength comes from Him.

That he had always been governed by love, without selfish views; and that having resolved to make the love of God the *end* of all his actions, he had found reasons to be well satisfied with his method.

That he was pleased when he could take up a straw from the ground for the love of God, seeking Him only, and nothing else, not even His gifts.

To what degree is love your governing thought? How are your days characterized by the love of God?

Ask God for a specific action of love you can carry out today. Then carry it out.

Do you still struggle to believe "It is finished"? What causes you to doubt the work God has already done on your behalf?

That he had been long troubled in mind from a certain belief that he should be damned; that all the men in the world could not have persuaded him to the contrary; but that he had thus reasoned with himself about it: *I engaged in a religious life only for the love of God, and I have endeavored to act only for Him; whatever becomes of me, whether I be lost or saved, I will always continue to act purely for the love of God. I shall have this good at least, that till death I shall have done all that is in me to love Him.* That this trouble of mind had lasted four years; during which time he had suffered much.

Spend time today in praying after ever greater faith in God; that He will reveal to you your "perfect liberty" and teach you His "continual joy."

But that at last he had seen that this trouble arose from want of faith; and that since then he had passed his life in perfect liberty and continual joy.

Today, confess. And then fully receive your forgiveness.

That he had placed his sins betwixt him and God, as it were, to tell Him that he did not deserve His favors, but that God still continued to bestow them in abundance.

Where do you sense He is calling you to greater "grit"
in your discipleship? How will that sharpen you?

That in order to form a habit of conversing with God continually, and referring all we do to Him, we must at first apply to Him with some diligence: but that after a little care we should find His love inwardly excite us to it without any difficulty.

That he expected after the pleasant days God had given him, he should have his turn of pain and suffering; but that he was not uneasy about it, knowing very well, that as he could do nothing of himself, God would not fail to give him the strength to bear it.

Write out your greatest fear. Even if that fear should come to pass, where will God be? And HOW will He be?

That when an occasion of practicing some virtue offered, he addressed himself to God, saying, Lord, I cannot do this unless Thou enablest me: and that then he received strength more than sufficient.

At every definable break in your schedule today (before meetings, between appointments, leaving from one place for another, etc.), pray Brother Lawrence's short prayer from this reading. Write it down and keep it with you for a constant reminder.

List every failing and shortfall in yourself you can think of. Then write God's response to your confessing it. Accept that His forgiveness if His plan for your day today.

That when he had failed in his duty, he only confessed his fault, saying to God, *I shall never do otherwise, if You leave me to myself; it is You who must hinder my falling, and mend what is amiss.* That after this, he gave himself no further uneasiness about it.

Today, attempt to hold an ongoing, frank, simple conversation with God about everything. Nothing is too small for His ear to hear.

That we ought to act with God in the greatest simplicity, speaking to Him frankly and plainly, and imploring His assistance in our affairs, just as they happen.

Write, or simply remember, the time when God's assistance was most palpable to you. How is that memory an encouragement to this day, today?

That God never failed to grant [His assistance], as he had often experienced.

What exact action or decision in your life is God calling you to absolutely surrender to Him and to His abilities?

That he had been lately sent into Burgundy, to buy the provision of wine for the society, which was a very unwelcome task for him, because he had no turn for business, and because he was lame and could not go about the boat but by rolling himself over the casks. That, however, he gave himself no uneasiness about it, nor about the purchase of the wine. That he said to God, *It was His business he was about*, and that he afterwards found it very well performed. That he had been sent into Auvergne, the year before, upon the same account; that he could not tell how the matter passed, but that it proved very well.

What do you hate to do the most? How might you meet God in that place? How have you already met God in that place?

So, likewise, in his business in the kitchen (to which he had naturally a great aversion), having accustomed himself to do everything there for the love of God, and with prayer, upon all occasions, for His grace to do his work well, he had found everything easy, during fifteen years that he had been employed there.

Write out the story of the stages of your life in bullet points. Meditate on the ways God made the divine connections from point to point.

That he was very well pleased with the post he was now in; but that he was as ready to quit that as the former, since he was always pleasing himself in every condition, by doing little things for the love of God.

That with him the set times of prayer were not different from other times; that he retired to pray, according to the directions of his Superior, but that he did not want such retirement, nor ask for it, because his greatest business did not divert him from God.

That as he knew his obligation to love God in all things, and as he endeavored so to do, he had no need of a director to advise him, but that he needed much a Confessor to absolve him.

Do you have a short repeatable prayer that is just yours— something you can happily intone no matter the time or setting? If so, write it below and enjoy utilizing it all day. If not, take time to write one for yourself.

Who is the friend with whom you can honestly share your struggles? Do you need to make some time to be with them and share any present challenges?

How long does it take you, after confessing your faults to God, to return to peace and joy? An indeterminate amount of time? A week? A day? An hour? Just a second?

Attempt to "think your thoughts to God" all day today. Seek not your own counsel and its anxieties. Notate below on the experience of contemplating Godward.

That he was very sensible of his faults, but not discouraged by them; that he confessed them to God, but did not plead against Him to excuse them. When he had so done, he peaceably resumed his usual practice of love and adoration.

That in his trouble of mind, he had consulted nobody, but knowing only by the light of faith that God was present, he contented himself with directing all his actions to Him, i.e., doing them with a desire to please Him, let what would come of it.

What is the most valueless thing you consistently give your thoughts to? Is it time to consciously let that go?

That useless thoughts spoil all: that the mischief began there; but that we ought to reject them, as soon as we perceived their impertinence to the matter in hand, or our salvation; and return to our communion with God.

To stem the potential today of wandering thoughts in prayer, use the space below to write a straightforward prayer from your heart. Use the simple language Brother Lawrence always reminds us to use.

_____

_____

_____

_____

_____

_____

_____

That at the beginning he had often passed his time appointed for prayer, in rejecting wandering thoughts, and falling back into them. That he could never regulate his devotion by certain methods as some do. That nevertheless, at first he had meditated for some time, but afterwards that went off, in a manner he could give no account of.

What are your present devotional practices and, honestly, how useful are they? Do they cause encounter with God—or are they simply boxes to check?

That all bodily mortifications and other exercises are useless, except as they serve to arrive at the union with God by love; that he had well considered this, and found it the shortest way to go straight to Him by a continual exercise of love, and doing all things for His sake.

Is it time for a change?

If so, to what?

What is one thing you will WILL for God's purposes today?

That we ought to make a great difference between the acts of the understanding and those of the will: that the first were comparatively of little value, and the others, all.

Pray for one way you can "delight yourself" in the Lord today. Then, do that.

That our only business was to love and delight ourselves in God.

That all possible kinds of mortification, if they were void of the love of God, could not efface a single sin. That we ought, without anxiety, to expect the pardon of our sins from the Blood of Jesus Christ, only endeavoring to love Him with all our hearts.

Write out precisely what you believe the Cross of Jesus has done for you. Do you only "know" this—or do you BELIEVE it?

List the "favors" God has granted you of which you are most readily aware. What do you they tell you about His regard for you?

That God seemed to have granted the greatest favors to the greatest sinners, as more signal monuments of His mercy.

What was the greatest spiritual pain you have ever experienced?

That the greatest pains or pleasures of this world, were not to be compared with what he had experienced of both kinds in a spiritual state: so that he was careful for nothing and feared nothing, desiring only one thing of God, viz., that he might not offend Him.

What was the greatest spiritual pleasure you have ever experienced?

What is God giving you strength for today? Are you ready to go perform that work?

That he had no scruples; for, said he, when I *fail* in my duty, I readily acknowledge it, saying, *I am used to do so: I shall never do otherwise, if I am left to myself.* I fail not, then I give God thanks, acknowledging the strength comes from Him.

Third Conversation

HE TOLD ME THAT the *foundation of the spiritual life* in *him*, had been a high notion and esteem of God in faith; which when he had once well conceived, he had no other care at first, but faithfully to reject every other thought, *that he might perform all his actions for the love of God*. That when sometimes he had not thought of God for a good while, he did not disquiet himself for it; but after having acknowledged his wretchedness to God, he returned to Him with so much the greater trust in Him, as he had found himself wretched through forgetting Him.

That the trust we put in God, honors Him much, and draws down great graces.

That it was impossible, not only that God should deceive, but also that He should long let a soul suffer which is perfectly resigned to Him, and resolved to endure everything for His sake.

That he had so often experienced the ready succors of Divine Grace upon all occasions, that from the same experience, when he had business to do, he did not think of it beforehand; but when it was time to do it, he found in God, as in a clear mirror, all that was fit for him to do. That of late he had acted thus, without anticipating care; but before the experience above mentioned, he had used it in his affairs.

When outward business diverted him a little from the thought of God, a fresh remembrance coming from God invested his soul, and so inflamed and transported him that it was difficult for him to contain himself.

That he was more united to God in his outward employments, than when he left them for devotion in retirement.

That he expected hereafter some great pain of body or mind; that the worst that could happen to him was, to lose that sense of God which he had enjoyed so long; but that the goodness of God assured him He would not forsake him utterly, and that He would give him strength to bear whatever evil He permitted to happen to him; and therefore that he feared nothing, and had no occasion to consult with anybody about his state. That when he had attempted to do it, he had always come away more perplexed; and that as he was conscious of his readiness to lay down his life for the love of God, he had no apprehension of danger. That perfect resignation to God was a sure way to heaven, a way in which we had always sufficient light for our conduct.

That in the beginning of the spiritual life, we ought to be faithful in doing our duty and denying ourselves; but after that, unspeakable pleasures followed; that in difficulties we need only have recourse to Jesus Christ, and beg His grace; with that everything became easy.

That many do not advance in the Christian progress because they stick in penances, and particular exercises, while they neglect the love of God, which is the *end*. That this appeared plainly by their works, and was the *reason* why we see so little solid virtue.

That there needed neither art nor science for going to God, but only a heart resolutely determined to apply itself to nothing but Him, or for *His* sake, and to love Him only.

What is an attribute of God about which you are currently learning? How will that impact the way you live your life today?

Spend today attempting this constant connecting with God. When you forget Him, don't despair; come right back with trust!

He told me that the *foundation of the spiritual life* in *him*, had been a high notion and esteem of God in faith; which when he had once well conceived, he had no other care at first, but faithfully to reject every other thought, *that he might perform all his actions for the love of God.*

That when sometimes he had not thought of God for a good while, he did not disquiet himself for it; but after having acknowledged his wretchedness to God, he returned to Him with so much the greater trust in Him, as he had found himself wretched through forgetting Him.

That the trust we put in God, honors Him much, and draws down great graces.

Your little life matters to God. Your obedience honors Him. His grace is yours.

What sort of day might you have, believing those three truths?

What is a current cause of suffering for you? Set aside time today to set it before God, resigning yourself to His love and protection, letting Him do an inner work in you.

That it was impossible, not only that God should deceive, but also that He should long let a soul suffer which is perfectly resigned to Him, and resolved to endure everything for His sake. That he had so often experienced the ready succors of Divine Grace upon all occasions, that from the same experience, when he had business to do, he did not think of it beforehand; but when it was time to do it, he found in God, as in a clear mirror, all that was fit for him to do. That of late he had acted thus, without anticipating care; but before the experience above mentioned, he had used it in his affairs.

Do an activity today that you believe will lead to an ecstatic experience of the presence of God. Write about the result.

When outward business diverted him a little from the thought of God, a fresh remembrance coming from God invested his soul, and so inflamed and transported him that it was difficult for him to contain himself.

Write out your schedule for the day ahead. Meditate before God on the ways He might want you to unite with Him in the midst of those scheduled events. Ask Him for specificity. Then live it.

That he was more united to God in his outward employments, than when he left them for devotion in retirement.

That he expected hereafter some great pain of body or mind; that the worst that could happen to him was, to lose that sense of God which he had enjoyed so long; but that the goodness of God assured him He would not forsake him utterly, and that He would give him strength to bear whatever evil He permitted to happen to him; and therefore that he feared nothing, and had no occasion to consult with anybody about his state.

What is your favorite promise of God from the scriptures? Write it out; meditate on it. How do its words encourage your outlook on this day in Him?

Are there any pieces of bad spiritual advice you've received and been living by? Discard anything that doesn't accord with the Way of Jesus!

That when he had attempted to [consult others about his inner life], he had always come away more perplexed; and that as he was conscious of his readiness to lay down his life for the love of God, he had no apprehension of danger.

Make a list of the glories you anticipate to meet in Heaven. How are you meant to be experiencing foretastes of those glories today?

That perfect resignation to God was a sure way to heaven, a way in which we had always sufficient light for our conduct.

*What is one act of clear, obedient faithfulness
God is asking you to perform? Will you?*

That in the beginning of the spiritual life, we ought to be faithful in doing our duty and denying ourselves; but after that, unspeakable pleasures followed....

...that in difficulties we need only have recourse to Jesus Christ, and beg His grace; with that everything became easy.

Is your life with Jesus easy or hard? Why do you answer that way?

Pick out one person in your life who sees you a great deal. Below, write out the way you think they would describe your life in Christ.

_____
_____
_____
_____
_____
_____

Spend time today in going after loving God only. Stoke the fires of affection!

That many do not advance in the Christian progress because they stick in penances, and particular exercises, while they neglect the love of God, which is the *end*. That this appeared plainly by their works, and was the *reason* why we see so little solid virtue.

That there needed neither art nor science for going to God, but only a heart resolutely determined to apply itself to nothing but Him, or for *His* sake, and to love Him only.

Fourth Conversation

HE DISCOURSED WITH ME very frequently, and with great openness of heart concerning his manner of *going* to God, whereof some part is related already.

He told me that all consists *in one hearty renunciation* of everything which we are sensible does not lead to God; that we might accustom ourselves to a continual conversation with Him, with freedom and in simplicity. That we need only to recognize God intimately present with us, to address ourselves to Him every moment, that we may beg His assistance for knowing His will in things doubtful, and for rightly performing those which we plainly see He requires of us, offering them to Him before we do them, and giving Him thanks when we have done.

That in this conversation with God, we are also employed in praising, adoring and loving Him incessantly, for His infinite goodness and perfection.

That, without being discouraged on account of our sins, we should pray for His grace with a perfect confidence, as relying upon the infinite merits of our Lord Jesus Christ. That God never failed offering us His grace at each action; that he distinctly perceived it, and never failed of it, unless when his thoughts had wandered from a sense of God's Presence, or he had forgotten to ask His assistance.

That God always gave us light in our doubts, when we had no other design but ask to please Him.

That our sanctification did not depend upon *changing* our works, but in doing that for God's sake, which we commonly do for our own. That it was lamentable to see how many people mistook the means for the end, addicting themselves to certain works, which they performed very imperfectly, by reason of their human or selfish regards.

That the most excellent method he had found of going to God, was that of doing our common business without any view of pleasing men[1], and (as far as we are capable) purely for the love of God.

That it was a great delusion to think that the times of prayer ought to differ from other times: that we are as strictly obliged to adhere to God by action in the time of action, as by prayer in the season of prayer.

That his prayer was nothing else but a sense of the presence of God, his soul being at that time insensible to everything but Divine love: and that when the appointed times of prayer were past, he found no difference, because he still continued with God, praising and blessing Him with all his might, so that he passed his life in continual joy; yet hoped that God would give him somewhat to suffer, when he should grow stronger.

That we ought, once for all, heartily to put our whole trust in God, and make a total surrender of ourselves to Him, secure that He would not deceive us.

That we ought not to be weary of doing little things for the love of God, who regards not the greatness of the work, but the love with which it is performed. That we should not wonder if, in the beginning, we often failed in our endeavors, but that at last we should gain a habit, which will naturally produce its acts in us, without our care, and to our exceeding great delight.

That the whole substance of religion was faith, hope and charity; by the practice of which we become united to the will of God: that all besides is indifferent, and to be used as a means that we may arrive at our end, and be swallowed up therein, by faith and charity.

That all things are possible to him who *believes*—that they are less difficult to him who *hopes*—that they are more easy to him who *loves*, and still more easy to him who perseveres in the practice of these three virtues.

That the end we ought to propose to ourselves is to become, in this life, the most perfect worshippers of God we can possibly be, as we hope to be through all eternity.

That when we enter upon the spiritual life, we should consider, and examine to the bottom, what we are. And then we should find ourselves worthy of all contempt, and not deserving indeed the name of Christians: subject to all kinds of misery and numberless accidents, which trouble us and cause perpetual vicissitudes in our health, in our humors, in our internal and external

---

1 Gal. i, 10; Eph. vi, 5, 6.

dispositions; in fine, persons whom God would humble by many pains and labors, as well within as without. After this we should not wonder that troubles, temptations, oppositions and contradictions happen to us from men. We ought, on the contrary, to submit ourselves to them, and bear them as long as God pleases, as things highly advantageous to us.

That the greater perfection a soul aspires after, the more dependent it is upon Divine grace.

[2]Being questioned by one of his own society (to whom he was obliged to open himself) by what means he had attained such an habitual sense of God, he told him that, since his first coming to the monastery, he had considered God as the end of all his thoughts and desires, as the mark to which they should tend, and in which they should terminate.

That in the beginning of his novitiate, he spent the hours appointed for private prayer in thinking of God, so as to convince his mind of, and to impress deeply upon his heart, the Divine existence, rather by devout sentiments, and submission to the lights of faith, than by studied reasonings and elaborate meditations. That by this short and sure method, he exercised himself in the knowledge and love of God, resolving to use his utmost endeavor to live, in a continual sense of His Presence, and if possible, never to forget Him more.

That when he had thus in prayer filled his mind with great sentiments of that infinite Being, he went to his work appointed in the kitchen (for he was cook to the society); there having first considered severally the things his office required, and when and how each thing was to be done, he spent all the intervals of his time, as well before as after his work, in prayer.

That when he began his business, he said to God, with a filial trust in Him, "O my God, since Thou art with me, and I must now, in obedience to Thy commands, apply my mind to these outward things, I beseech Thee to grant me the grace to continue in Thy Presence; and to this end do Thou prosper me with Thy assistance, receive all my works, and possess all my affections."

As he proceeded in his work, he continued his familiar conversation with his Maker—imploring His grace, and offering to Him all his actions.

When he had finished, he examined himself how he had discharged his duty; if he found *well*, he returned thanks to God; if otherwise, he asked pardon; and without being discouraged, he set his mind right again, and continued his

---

[2] The particulars which follow are collected from other accounts of Brother Lawrence.

exercise of the *presence* of God, as if he had never deviated from it. "Thus," said he, "by rising after my falls, and by frequently renewed acts of faith and love, I am come to a state wherein it would be as difficult for me not to think of God as it was at first to accustom myself to it."

As brother Lawrence had found such an advantage in walking in the presence of God, it was natural for him to recommend it earnestly to others; but his example was a stronger inducement than any arguments he could propose. His very countenance was edifying, such a sweet and calm devotion appearing in it as could not but effect the beholders. And it was observed that in the greatest hurry of business in the kitchen, he still preserved his recollection and heavenly-mindedness. He was never hasty nor loitering, but did each thing in its season, with an even, uninterrupted composure and tranquility of spirit. "The time of business," said he, "does not with me differ from the time of prayer; and in the noise and clatter of my kitchen, while several persons are at the same time calling for different things, I possess God in as great tranquility as if I were upon my knees at the blessed sacrament."

If a brother or sister in Christ asked you how you "go to God," what would be your present answer?

What do you need to renounce—once and forever?

He discoursed with me very frequently, and with great openness of heart concerning his manner of *going* to God, whereof some part is related already.

He told me that all consists *in one hearty renunciation* of everything which we are sensible does not lead to God; that we might accustom ourselves to a continual conversation with Him, with freedom and in simplicity.

That we need only to recognize God intimately present with us, to address ourselves to Him every moment, that we may beg His assistance for knowing His will in things doubtful, and for rightly performing those which we plainly see He requires of us, offering them to Him before we do them, and giving Him thanks when we have done.

Set an alarm in your day today when you know your day will be most fraught and full. When that alarm sounds, stop everything and worship God with your all.

That in this conversation with God, we are also employed in praising, adoring and loving Him incessantly, for His infinite goodness and perfection.

Pick a worship song you're presently enjoying and sing it all the way through to Him. Enjoy!

List as many things you love about Jesus as you can conjure. Which presently stands out most?

That, without being discouraged on account of our sins, we should pray for His grace with a perfect confidence, as relying upon the infinite merits of our Lord Jesus Christ.

Spend today paying attention to the manifold graces of God upon your life.

That God never failed offering us His grace at each action; that he distinctly perceived it, and never failed of it, unless when his thoughts had wandered from a sense of God's Presence, or he had forgotten to ask His assistance.

That God always gave us light in our doubts, when we had no other design but ask to please Him.

What is a doubt about God you're presently harboring? What light might He bring to that?

That our sanctification did not depend upon *changing* our works, but in doing that for God's sake, which we commonly do for our own.

What is one action in your life you could "convert" from yours to His?

What are "meaningless" things that you readily see others doing? Why do you think these actions bother you? (Do they perhaps live in your own heart too?)

That it was lamentable to see how many people mistook the means for the end, addicting themselves to certain works, which they performed very imperfectly, by reason of their human or selfish regards.

That the most excellent method he had found of going to God, was that of doing our common business without any view of pleasing men[3], and (as far as we are capable) purely for the love of God.

Who is the one person in your life that you most worry about pleasing? Why? Is it time for that to change? How?

---

3   Gal. i, 10; Eph. vi, 5, 6.

That it was a great delusion to think that the times of prayer ought to differ from other times: that we are as strictly obliged to adhere to God by action in the time of action, as by prayer in the season of prayer.

Today—morning, noon and night—stop everything you are doing and spend time enjoying God. Let your whole heart be in His direction.

Sit in perfect stillness and wait upon the manifest presence of God.

That his prayer was nothing else but a sense of the presence of God, his soul being at that time insensible to everything but Divine love: and that when the appointed times of prayer were past, he found no difference, because he still continued with God, praising and blessing Him with all his might, so that he passed his life in continual joy; yet hoped that God would give him somewhat to suffer, when he should grow stronger.

Take a walk today and talk to God about trust, surrender, security in Him. Record your reflections afterward.

That we ought, once for all, heartily to put our whole trust in God, and make a total surrender of ourselves to Him, secure that He would not deceive us.

Do one little loving act for His purposes today. Tell no one. Enjoy its intimacy only with Him.

That we ought not to be weary of doing little things for the love of God, who regards not the greatness of the work, but the love with which it is performed.

List the helpful habits you've created between yourself and God. Then rank them, most fruitful to least fruitful, and consider their spiritual benefit to you.

That we should not wonder if, in the beginning, we often failed in our endeavors, but that at last we should gain a habit, which will naturally produce its acts in us, without our care, and to our exceeding great delight.

How do you presently carry out the personal work of "charity"? How might the Lord be wanting to change that—or increase it?

That the whole substance of religion was faith, hope and charity; by the practice of which we become united to the will of God: that all besides is indifferent, and to be used as a means that we may arrive at our end, and be swallowed up therein, by faith and charity.

Define for yourself the meaning of each of Brother Lawrence's categories:

"belief" –

"hope" –

"love" –

> That all things are possible to him who *believes*—that they are less difficult to him who *hopes*—that they are more easy to him who *loves*, and still more easy to him who perseveres in the practice of these three virtues.

Spend a day in constant pursuit of a higher sense of worship. Worship however God instructs you to.

That the end we ought to propose to ourselves is to become, in this life, the most perfect worshippers of God we can possibly be, as we hope to be through all eternity.

Write an honest self-assessment of your faults. For each, pray about and then notate on what God is attempting to do IN YOU right now. How is He changing you, through your faults, FROM WITHIN?

That when we enter upon the spiritual life, we should consider, and examine to the bottom, what we are. And then we should find ourselves worthy of all contempt, and not deserving indeed the name of Christians: subject to all kinds of misery and numberless accidents, which trouble us and cause perpetual vicissitudes in our health, in our humors, in our internal and external dispositions; in fine, persons whom God would humble by many pains and labors, as well within as without.

Who are you presently called to "turn the other cheek" to? Who in your life are you meant to love because of the way their enmity is shaping you?

After this we should not wonder that troubles, temptations, oppositions and contradictions happen to us from men. We ought, on the contrary, to submit ourselves to them, and bear them as long as God pleases, as things highly advantageous to us.

Ask God where He is presently, most actively working to "perfect" you? How are you helping or hindering Him in that place?

That the greater perfection a soul aspires after, the more dependent it is upon Divine grace.

[4]Being questioned by one of his own society (to whom he was obliged to open himself) by what means he had attained such an habitual sense of God, he told him that, since his first coming to the monastery, he had considered God as the end of all his thoughts and desires, as the mark to which they should tend, and in which they should terminate.

Write out today's schedule—so far as you know it. Spend time praying for experience of God's presence in each of those parts of your day.

---

4   The particulars which follow are collected from other accounts of Brother Lawrence.

Today, set a time for 15 minutes in which to silently sit before God. Think of Him, talk to Him, listen to Him, delight to be still and alone with Him.

What did you experience in your 15 minutes yesterday? How might that experience inform your living of this day?

That in the beginning of his novitiate, he spent the hours appointed for private prayer in thinking of God, so as to convince his mind of, and to impress deeply upon his heart, the Divine existence, rather by devout sentiments, and submission to the lights of faith, than by studied reasonings and elaborate meditations.

That by this short and sure method [of simply thinking about God Himself], he exercised himself in the knowledge and love of God, resolving to use his utmost endeavor to live, in a continual sense of His Presence, and if possible, never to forget Him more.

That when he had thus in prayer filled his mind with great sentiments of that infinite Being, he went to his work appointed in the kitchen (for he was cook to the society); there having first considered severally the things his office required, and when and how each thing was to be done, he spent all the intervals of his time, as well before as after his work, in prayer.

List every action you can imagine yourself carrying out today, sequentially. Ask God for how to honor Him in each and every one.

Rewrite Brother Lawrence's prayer in your own words—and spend time praying it.

That when he began his business, he said to God, with a filial trust in Him, "O my God, since Thou art with me, and I must now, in obedience to Thy commands, apply my mind to these outward things, I beseech Thee to grant me the grace to continue in Thy Presence; and to this end do Thou prosper me with Thy assistance, receive all my works, and possess all my affections."

As he proceeded in his work, he continued his familiar conversation with his Maker,—imploring His grace, and offering to Him all his actions.

Saturate the course of today in prayer. Bring God into every situation and every situation into the presence of God.

When he had finished, he examined himself how he had discharged his duty; if he found *well*, he returned thanks to God; if otherwise, he asked pardon; and without being discouraged, he set his mind right again, and continued his exercise of the *presence* of God, as if he had never deviated from it.

Reflect on yesterday's experience of practicing the presence. List out the "highs and lows." Return thanks; ask pardon; set your mind right again; continue the exercise in this day.

When was the hour of your greatest fall? How did God lift you up and restore you?

"Thus," said he, "by rising after my falls, and by frequently renewed acts of faith and love, I am come to a state wherein it would be as difficult for me not to think of God as it was at first to accustom myself to it."

As Brother Lawrence had found such an advantage in walking in the presence of God, it was natural for him to recommend it earnestly to others; but his example was a stronger inducement than any arguments he could propose.

Who mentors you? Who do you mentor? The Kingdom of Heaven grows by the depth of our discipleship and discipling!

His very countenance was edifying, such a sweet and calm devotion appearing in it as could not but effect the beholders. And it was observed that in the greatest hurry of business in the kitchen, he still preserved his recollection and heavenly-mindedness.

What will be the single most stressful part of the day before you? Imagine it—and pray about how your countenance might appear to others during it.

What element of your regular life feels least like a blessed sacrament? How might God want you to open that place to His presence?

He was never hasty nor loitering, but did each thing in its season, with an even, uninterrupted composure and tranquility of spirit. "The time of business," said he, "does not with me differ from the time of prayer; and in the noise and clatter of my kitchen, while several persons are at the same time calling for different things, I possess God in as great tranquility as if I were upon my knees at the blessed sacrament."

First Letter

SINCE YOU DESIRE so earnestly that I should communicate to you the method by which I arrived at that *habitual sense of God's Presence*, which our Lord, of His mercy, has been pleased to vouch-safe to me, I must tell you that it is with great difficulty that I am prevailed on by your importunities; and now I do it only upon the terms that you show my letter to nobody. If I knew that you should let it be seen, all the desire that I have for your advancement would not be able to determine me to it. The account I can give you is:

Having found in many books different methods of going to God, and divers practices of the spiritual life, I thought this would serve rather to puzzle me than facilitate what I sought after, which was nothing but how to become wholly God's. This made me resolve to give the all for the all; so after having given myself wholly to God, that He might take away my sin, *I renounced, for the love of Him, everything that was not He; and I began to live as if there was none but He and I in the world*. Sometimes I considered myself before Him as a poor criminal at the feet of his judge; at other times I beheld Him in my heart as my Father, as my God: I worshipped Him the oftenest that I could, keeping my mind in His holy Presence, and recalling it as often as I found it wandered from Him. I found no small pain in this exercise, and yet I continued it, notwithstanding all the difficulties that occurred, without troubling or disquieting myself when my mind had wandered involuntarily. I made this my business as much all the day long as at the appointed times of prayer; for at all times, every hour, every minute, even in the height of my business, I drove away from my mind everything that was capable of interrupting my thought of God.

 Such has been my common practice ever since I entered in religion; and, though I have done it very imperfectly, yet I have found great advantages by it. These, I well know, are to be imputed to the mere mercy and goodness of God, because we can do nothing without Him; and *I* still less than any. But when we are faithful to keep ourselves in His holy Presence, and set Him always before us, this not only hinders our offending Him, and doing anything that may displease Him, at least wilfully, but it also begets in us a holy freedom, and, if I may so speak, a familiarity with God, wherewith we ask, and that successfully, the graces we stand in need of. In fine, by often repeating these acts, they become *habitual*, and the presence of God rendered as it were *natural to* us. Give Him thanks, if you please, with me, for His great goodness towards me, which I can never sufficiently admire, for the many favors He has done to so miserable a sinner as I am. May all things praise Him. Amen.

 I am, in our Lord, yours, &c.

Draw a pie-chart that shows the percentage of your "true life" that is external vs. internal.

Since you desire so earnestly that I should communicate to you the method by which I arrived at that *habitual sense of God's Presence*, which our Lord, of His mercy, has been pleased to vouch-safe to me, I must tell you that it is with great difficulty that I am prevailed on by your importunities; and now I do it only upon the terms that you show my letter to nobody. If I knew that you should let it be seen, all the desire that I have for your advancement would not be able to determine me to it.

The account I can give you is: Having found in many books different methods of going to God, and divers practices of the spiritual life, I thought this would serve rather to puzzle me than facilitate what I sought after, which was nothing but how to become wholly God's. This made me resolve to give the all for the all; so after having given myself wholly to God, that He might take away my sin, *I renounced, for the love of Him, everything that was not He; and I began to live as if there was none but He and I in the world.*

In your whole life, when was the presence of God most palpable to you?

Describe the image in your mind when you think of God. If it helps, draw or sketch it.

Sometimes I considered myself before Him as a poor criminal at the feet of his judge; at other times I beheld Him in my heart as my Father, as my God: I worshipped Him the oftenest that I could, keeping my mind in His holy Presence, and recalling it as often as I found it wandered from Him.

Do you believe that your drawing near to Him brings God pleasure? How does that thought impact your desire to get even closer?

I found no small pain in this exercise [of keeping his mind stayed on God], and yet I continued it, notwithstanding all the difficulties that occurred, without troubling or disquieting myself when my mind had wandered involuntarily.

What is a nagging worry that is haunting your mind today?

I made this my business as much all the day long as at the appointed times of prayer; for at all times, every hour, every minute, even in the height of my business, I drove away from my mind everything that was capable of interrupting my thought of God.

When you think of your life "before God" and "since God," what are the greatest differences? How would you explain them to a non-believer?

Such has been my common practice ever since I entered in religion; and, though I have done it very imperfectly, yet I have found great advantages by it. These, I well know, are to be imputed to the mere mercy and goodness of God, because we can do nothing without Him; and *I* still less than any.

Do you consider God to be your friend? Why do you answer that way?

But when we are faithful to keep ourselves in His holy Presence, and set Him always before us, this not only hinders our offending Him, and doing anything that may displease Him, at least wilfully, but it also begets in us a holy freedom, and, if I may so speak, a familiarity with God, wherewith we ask, and that successfully, the graces we stand in need of.

How is the presence of God more "natural" for you since starting this journey with Brother Lawrence? Where do you feel you still need to grow in your personal experience?

In fine, by often repeating these acts, they become *habitual*, and the presence of God rendered as it were *natural to us*.

What is your favorite place in the Psalms? Go remind yourself and record it here.

Give Him thanks, if you please, with me, for His great goodness towards me, which I can never sufficiently admire, for the many favors He has done to so miserable a sinner as I am. May all things praise Him. Amen.

Second Letter
To the Reverend—

NOT FINDING MY MANNER of life in books, although I have no difficulty about it, yet, for greater security, I shall be glad to know your thoughts concerning it.

In a conversation some days since with a person of piety, he told me the spiritual life was a life of grace, which begins with servile fear, which is increased by hope of eternal life, and which is consummated by pure love. That each of these states had its different stages, by which one arrives at last at that blessed consummation.

I have not followed all these methods. On the contrary, from I know not what instincts, I found they discouraged me. This was the reason why, at my entrance into religion, I took a resolution to give myself up to God, as the best return I could make for His love; and, for the love of Him, to renounce all besides.

For the first year I commonly employed myself during the time set apart for devotion with the thought of death, judgment, heaven, hell, and my sins, Thus continued some years, applying my mind carefully the rest of the day, and even in the midst of my business, *to the presence of God*, whom I considered always as *with* me, often as *in* me.

At length I came insensibly to do the same thing during my set time of prayer, which caused in me great delight and consolation. This practice produced in me so high an esteem for God, that *faith* alone was capable to satisfy me in that point.[5]

Such was my beginning; and yet I must tell you that for the first ten years I suffered much: the apprehension that I was not devoted to God as I wished to be, my past sins always present to my mind, and the great unmerited favors which God did me, were the matter and source of my sufferings. During this time I fell often, and rose again presently. It seemed to me that all creatures, reason, and God Himself were against me; and *faith* alone for me. I was troubled sometimes with thoughts that to believe I had received such favors was an effect of my presumption, which pretended to be *at once* where others arrive with difficulty; at other times that it was a wilful delusion, and that there was no salvation for me.

When I thought of nothing but to end my days in these troubles (which did not at all diminish the trust I had in God, and which served only to increase my faith), I found myself changed all at once; and my soul, which, till that time, was in trouble, felt a profound inward peace, as if she were in her centre and place of rest.

Ever since that time I walk before God simply, in faith, with humility and with love; and I apply myself diligently to do nothing and think nothing which may displease Him. I hope that when I have done what I can, He will do with me what He pleases.

As for what passes in me at present, I cannot express it. I have no pain or difficulty about my state, because I have no will but that of God, which I endeavor to accomplish in all things, and to which I am so resigned that I would not take up a straw from the ground against His order, or from any other motive than purely that of love to Him.

I have quitted all forms of devotion and set prayers but those to which my state obliges me. And I make it my business only to persevere in His holy presence, wherein I keep myself by a simple attention, and a general fond regard to God, which I may call an *actual presence of God*; or, to speak better, an habitual, silent and secret conversation of the soul with God, which often causes me joys and raptures inwardly, and sometimes also outwardly, so great, that I am forced to use means to moderate them and prevent their appearance to others.

---

5 *I suppose he means* that all distinct notions he could form of God, were unsatisfactory, because he perceived them to be unworthy of God; and therefore his mind was not to be satisfied but by the views of *faith*, which apprehend God as infinite and incomprehensible, as He is in Himself, and not as He can be conceived by human ideas.

In short, I am assured beyond all doubt that my soul has been with God above these thirty years. I pass over many things that I may not be tedious to you, yet I think it proper to inform you after what manner I consider myself before God, whom I behold as my King.

I consider myself as the most wretched of men, full of sores and corruption, and who has committed all sorts of crimes against his King; touched with a sensible regret, I confess to him all my wickedness, I ask His forgiveness, I abandon myself in His hands that He may do what He pleases with me. The King, full of mercy and goodness, very far from chastising me, embraces me with love, makes me eat at His table, serves me with His own hands, gives me the key of His treasures; He converses and delights Himself with me incessantly, in a thousand and a thousand ways, and treats me in all respects as His favorite. It is thus I consider myself from time to time in His holy presence.

My most useful method is this simple attention, and such a general passionate regard to God; to whom I find myself often attached with greater sweetness and delight than that of an infant at the mother's breast; so that, if I dare use the expression, I should choose to call this state the bosom, of God, for the inexpressible sweetness which I taste and experience there.

If sometimes my thoughts wander from it by necessity or infirmity, I am presently recalled by inward motions so charming and delicious that I am ashamed to mention them. I desire your reverence to reflect rather upon my great wretchedness, of which you are fully informed, than upon the great favors which God does me, all unworthy and ungrateful as I am.

As for my set hours of prayer, they are only a continuation of the same exercise. Sometimes I consider myself there as a stone before a carver, whereof he is to make a statue; presenting myself thus before God, I desire Him to form His perfect image in my soul, and make me entirely like Himself.

At other times, when I apply myself to prayer, I feel all my spirit and all my soul lift itself up without any care or effort of mine, and it continues as it were suspended and firmly fixed in God, as in its centre and place of rest.

I know that some charge this state with inactivity, delusion and self-love. I confess that it is a holy inactivity, and would be a happy self-love, if the soul in that state were capable of it; because, in effect, while she is in this repose, she cannot be disturbed by such acts as she was formerly accustomed to, and which were then her support, but which would now rather hinder than assist her.

Yet I cannot bear that this should be called delusion; because the soul which thus enjoys God desires herein nothing but Him. If this be delusion in me, it belongs to God to remedy it. Let Him do what He pleases with me; I desire only Him, and to be wholly devoted to Him. You will, however, oblige me in sending me your opinion, to which I always pay a great deference, for I have a singular esteem for your reverence, and am in our Lord,

Yours, &c.

*Who is a wise counselor you might seek out
to aid your spiritual journey?*

Not finding my manner of life in books, although I have no difficulty about it, yet, for greater security, I shall be glad to know your thoughts concerning it.

Seek them out.

...From I know not what instincts, I found [that others' way of following and knowing God] discouraged me. This was the reason why, at my entrance into religion, I took a resolution to give myself up to God, as the best return I could make for His love; and, for the love of Him, to renounce all besides.

Are there others whose spiritual journey—or advice about your own spiritual journey—has actually been a discouragement to you? Reflect on why that is.

Since Jesus has rendered to us the OPPOSITES *of "death, judgment...hell, and... sins"—ie. eternal life, freedom from judgment, Heaven itself, holy faultlessness—how will you live today? Where is your Savior living right now?*

For the first year I commonly employed myself during the time set apart for devotion with the thought of death, judgment, heaven, hell, and my sins. Thus continued some years, applying my mind carefully the rest of the day, and even in the midst of my business, *to the presence of God*, whom I considered always as *with* me, often as *in* me.

Focus your whole attention today on living in Jesus with "great delight and consolation." Let nothing sway you from this one focus.

At length I came insensibly to do the same thing during my set time of prayer, which caused in me great delight and consolation. This practice produced in me so high an esteem for God, that *faith* alone was capable to satisfy me in that point.

As you consider Brother Lawrence's list, in which place do you spend most of your time—

In worry that you are not devoted enough to God?

In the mire of the battle of sin—whether present or past?

In swimming in the "great unmerited favors" of God?

Such was my beginning; and yet I must tell you that for the first ten years I suffered much: the apprehension that I was not devoted to God as I wished to be, my past sins always present to my mind, and the great unmerited favors which God did me, were the matter and source of my sufferings. During this time I fell often, and rose again presently.

It seemed to me that all creatures, reason, and God Himself were against me; and *faith* alone for me. I was troubled sometimes with thoughts that to believe I had received such favors was an effect of my presumption, which pretended to be *at once* where others arrive with difficulty; at other times that it was a wilful delusion, and that there was no salvation for me.

List the first ten thoughts that filled your mind when you woke this morning. After, lay each before God.

If nothing can touch your life without God's knowledge—and God knows all—and promises that "all things work together for those who believe"—how should you live this day?

When I thought of nothing but to end my days in these troubles (which did not at all diminish the trust I had in God, and which served only to increase my faith), I found myself changed all at once; and my soul, which, till that time, was in trouble, felt a profound inward peace, as if she were in her centre and place of rest.

Ever since that time I walk before God simply, in faith, with humility and with love...

Before God, today, simply walk in faith, humility and love. Enjoy the nearness of His presence.

I apply myself diligently to do nothing and think nothing which may displease Him. I hope that when I have done what I can, He will do with me what He pleases.

List every part of yourself with which God is pleased. Remember: He is a loving Father and sees Jesus in you!

Spend a day praying through EVERY SINGLE DECISION *lying before you. Enjoy talking with God about* EVERY LITTLE THING.

What is the most robust part of your devotional life right now? What feels less fruitful? Why?

As for what passes in me at present, I cannot express it. I have no pain or difficulty about my state, because I have no will but that of God, which I endeavor to accomplish in all things, and to which I am so resigned that I would not take up a straw from the ground against His order, or from any other motive than purely that of love to Him.

I have quitted all forms of devotion and set prayers but those to which my state obliges me.

What is one act or action you could pursue today in the direction of ecstasy in the presence of God? Take that step.

I make it my business only to persevere in His holy presence, wherein I keep myself by a simple attention, and a general fond regard to God, which I may call an *actual presence of God*; or, to speak better, an habitual, silent and secret conversation of the soul with God, which often causes me joys and raptures inwardly, and sometimes also outwardly, so great, that I am forced to use means to moderate them and prevent their appearance to others.

If you were the personal servant of an earthly king, how would you conduct this day? What would be the actions required of you? List those.

Now remember that you are indeed the servant of THE King!

In short, I am assured beyond all doubt that my soul has been with God above these thirty years. I pass over many things that I may not be tedious to you, yet I think it proper to inform you after what manner I consider myself before God, whom I behold as my King.

I consider myself as the most wretched of men, full of sores and corruption, and who has committed all sorts of crimes against his King; touched with a sensible regret, I confess to him all my wickedness, I ask His forgiveness, I abandon myself in His hands that He may do what He pleases with me.

Be quick to confess all day today. Be mindful of where you fall short.

The King, full of mercy and goodness, very far from chastising me, embraces me with love, makes me eat at His table, serves me with His own hands, gives me the key of His treasures...

Be quick to receive forgiveness all day today. Be mindful of the magnitude of His grace and affection.

Write yourself a letter from God, knowing that you are "His favorite." Put yourself in the shoes of the One who loves you. What does He say to you?

He converses and delights Himself with me incessantly, in a thousand and a thousand ways, and treats me in all respects as His favorite. It is thus I consider myself from time to time in His holy presence.

My most useful method is this simple attention, and such a general passionate regard to God; to whom I find myself often attached with greater sweetness and delight than that of an infant at the mother's breast; so that, if I dare use the expression, I should choose to call this state the bosom of God, for the inexpressible sweetness which I taste and experience there.

Write a letter to God, sharing with Him your "passionate regard" for Him, letting Him know of the "sweetness and delight" of being His.

Write a description of your experience and knowledge of the inwardness of God, ie. His Holy Spirit.

If sometimes my thoughts wander from [the sweetness of God] by necessity or infirmity, I am presently recalled by inward motions so charming and delicious that I am ashamed to mention them.

As of today, make a copious list of God's "great favors" upon the whole of your life. Try to think of absolutely everything!

I desire your reverence to reflect rather upon my great wretchedness, of which you are fully informed, than upon the great favors which God does me, all unworthy and ungrateful as I am.

Draw a picture of how you view Jesus, the Father, the Holy Spirit. What does the presence of God conjure in your artistic imagination?

Today, take a long walk and simply be with God.

As for my set hours of prayer, they are only a continuation of the same exercise. Sometimes I consider myself there as a stone before a carver, whereof he is to make a statue; presenting myself thus before God, I desire Him to form His perfect image in my soul, and make me entirely like Himself.

At other times, when I apply myself to prayer, I feel all my spirit and all my soul lift itself up without any care or effort of mine, and it continues as it were suspended and firmly fixed in God, as in its centre and place of rest.

I know that some charge this state with inactivity, delusion and self-love. I confess that it is a holy inactivity, and would be a happy self-love, if the soul in that state were capable of it; because, in effect, while she is in this repose, she cannot be disturbed by such acts as she was formerly accustomed to, and which were then her support, but which would now rather hinder than assist her.

When are the times when you most "lose yourself" in God? Do whatever that is today!

Are you afraid of appearing "weird" for the sake of knowing God? Why do you think that is?

Yet I cannot bear that this should be called delusion; because the soul which thus enjoys God desires herein nothing but Him. If this be delusion in me, it belongs to God to remedy it.

Let Him do what He pleases with me; I desire only Him, and to be wholly devoted to Him.

Set aside some time today to simply sit before Him. Be silent. Desire Him. Let Him express His pleasure to you.

You will, however, oblige me in sending me your opinion, to which I always pay a great deference, for I have a singular esteem for your reverence....

Ask a trusted brother or sister for "a word" today. Let them express their own experience of God so that you may learn of it.

Third Letter

WE HAVE A GOD who is infinitely gracious and knows all our wants. I always thought that He would reduce you to extremity. He will come in His own time, and when you least expect it. Hope in Him more than ever; thank Him with me for the favors He does you, particularly for the fortitude and patience which He gives you in your afflictions. It is a plain mark of the care He takes of you. Comfort yourself, then, with Him, and give thanks for all.

I admire also the fortitude and bravery of Mr. ——. God has given him a good disposition and a good will; but there is in him still a little of the world, and a great deal of youth. I hope the affliction which God has sent him will prove a wholesome remedy to him, and make him enter into himself. It is an accident which should engage him to put all his trust in *Him* who accompanies him everywhere. Let him think of Him as often as he can, especially in the greatest dangers. A little lifting up of the heart suffices. A little remembrance of God, one act of inward worship, though upon a march, and a sword in hand, are prayers, which, however short, are nevertheless very acceptable to God; and far from lessening a soldier's courage in occasions of danger, they best serve to fortify it.

Let him then think of God the most he can. Let him accustom himself, by degrees, to this small but holy exercise. No one will notice it, and nothing is easier than to repeat often in the day these little internal adorations. Recommend to him, if you please, that he think of God the most he can, in the manner here directed. It is very fit and most necessary for a soldier, who is daily exposed to the dangers of life. I hope that God will assist him and all the family, to whom I present my service, being theirs and Yours, &c.

We have a God who is infinitely gracious and knows all our wants. I always thought that He would reduce you to extremity. He will come in His own time, and when you least expect it.

What is a desire of your heart that you have yet to lay before God?

Hope in Him more than ever; thank Him with me for the favors he does you, particularly for the fortitude and patience which He gives you in your afflictions. It is a plain mark of the care He takes of you. Comfort yourself, then, with Him, and give thanks for all.

Make a list of those parts of your life for which you feel thankful.

Remind yourself of a time in your life that felt tragic to you—and which God used for His high purposes.

I admire also the fortitude and bravery of Mr. ——. God has given him a good disposition and a good will; but there is in him still a little of the world, and a great deal of youth. I hope the affliction which God has sent him will prove a wholesome remedy to him, and make him enter into himself. It is an accident which should engage him to put all his trust in *Him* who accompanies him everywhere.

Let him think of Him as often as he can, especially in the greatest dangers. A little lifting up of the heart suffices. A little remembrance of God, one act of inward worship, though upon a march, and a sword in hand, are prayers, which, however short, are nevertheless very acceptable to God; and far from lessening a soldier's courage in occasions of danger, they best serve to fortify it.

What is the simple prayer of your heart this particular day?

Come up with a remembrance tool—a rubber band on your wrist, a pen-mark on your hand, a scarf around your neck—that will help you maintain a constancy of devotion today. Make use of this tool to keep you constantly in the presence, mindful of your God.

Let him then think of God the most he can. Let him accustom himself, by degrees, to this small but holy exercise. No one will notice it, and nothing is easier than to repeat often in the day these little internal adorations. Recommend to him, if you please, that he think of God the most he can, in the manner here directed. It is very fit and most necessary for a soldier, who is daily exposed to the dangers of life. I hope that God will assist him and all the family, to whom I present my service....

Fourth Letter

I HAVE TAKEN THIS opportunity to communicate to you the sentiments of one of our society, concerning the admirable effects and continual assistances which he receives from *the presence of God*. Let you and me both profit by them.

You must know his continual care has been, for about forty years past that he has spent in religion, to be *always with God*, and to do nothing, say nothing, and think nothing which may displease Him; and this without any other view than purely for the love of Him, and because He deserves infinitely more.

He is now so accustomed to that *Divine Presence*, that he receives from it continual succors upon all occasions. For about thirty years, his soul has been filled with joys so continual, and sometimes so great, that he is forced to use means to moderate them, and to hinder their appearing outwardly.

If sometimes he is a little too much absent from that *Divine Presence*, God presently makes Himself to be felt in his soul to recall Him, which often happens when he is most engaged in his outward business. He answers with exact fidelity to these inward drawings, either by an elevation of his heart towards God, or by a meek and fond regard to Him, or by such words as love forms upon these occasions, as for instance, *My God, here I am all devoted to Thee*: *Lord, make me according to Thy heart*. And then it seems to him (as in effect he feels it) that this God of love, satisfied with such few words, reposes again, and rests in the fund and centre of his soul. The experience of these things gives him such an assurance that God is always in the fund or bottom of his soul, that it renders him incapable of doubting it upon any account whatever.

Judge by this what content and satisfaction he enjoys while he continually finds in himself so great a treasure. He is no longer in an anxious search after it, but has it open before him, and may take what he pleases of it.

He complains much of our blindness, and cries often that we are to be pitied who content ourselves with so little. God, saith he, *has infinite treasure to bestow, and we take up with a little sensible devotion, which passes in a moment. Blind as we are, we hinder* God, *and stop the current of His graces. But when He finds a soul penetrated with a lively faith, He pours into it His graces and favors plentifully: there they flow like a torrent, which, after being forcibly stopped against its ordinary course, when it has found a passage, spreads itself with impetuosity and abundance.*

Yes, we often stop this torrent by the little value we set upon it. But let us stop it no more; let us enter into ourselves and break down the bank which hinders it. Let us make way for grace; let us redeem the lost time, for perhaps we have but little left. Death follows us close; let us be well prepared for it: for we die but once; and a miscarriage *there* is irretrievable.

I say again, let us enter into ourselves. The time presses, there is no room for delay: our souls are at stake. I believe you have taken such effectual measures that you will not be surprised. I commend you for it; it is the one thing necessary. We must, nevertheless, always work at it, because not to advance in the spiritual life is to go back. But those who have the gale of the Holy Spirit go forward even in sleep. If the vessel of our soul is still tossed with winds and storms, let us awake the Lord, who reposes in it, and He will quickly calm the sea.

I have taken the liberty to impart to you these good sentiments, that you may compare them with your own. It will serve again to kindle and inflame them, if by misfortune (which God forbid, for it would be indeed a great misfortune) they should be, though never so little, cooled. Let us then *both* recall our first fervors. Let us profit by the example and the sentiments of this brother, who is little known of the world, but known of God, and extremely caressed by Him. I will pray for you; do you pray instantly for me, who am, in our Lord.

Yours, &c.

Share a recent spiritual learning of yours with a friend. Ask for his/hers. Take heart in your spiritual fellowship together.

Write a love poem to God. Express your heart rapturously.

I have taken this opportunity to communicate to you the sentiments of one of our society, concerning the admirable effects and continual assistances which he receives from *the presence of God*. Let you and me both profit by them.

You must know his continual care has been, for about forty years past that he has spent in religion, to be *always with God*, and to do nothing, say nothing, and think nothing which may displease Him; and this without any other view than purely for the love of Him, and because He deserves infinitely more.

He is now so accustomed to that *Divine Presence*, that he receives from it continual succors upon all occasions.

Set an hourly timer on your phone or watch for the day today. At each alarm, pause in God's presence and receive reminder of His goodness.

For about thirty years, his soul has been filled with joys so continual, and sometimes so great, that he is forced to use means to moderate them, and to hinder their appearing outwardly.

At some point today, put on your favorite worship song and SHOUT YOUR PRAISE to God!

At the time in your day when you are confronting the most stress and decision-making:

Stop

Smile to yourself

That is the moment when God is holding you

Right now, what part of yourself would you most want God to remold?

If sometimes he is a little too much absent from that *Divine Presence*, God presently makes Himself to be felt in his soul to recall Him, which often happens when he is most engaged in his outward business.

He answers with exact fidelity to these inward drawings, either by an elevation of his heart towards God, or by a meek and fond regard to Him, or by such words as love forms upon these occasions, as for instance, *My God, here I am all devoted to Thee: Lord, make me according to Thy heart.*

And then it seems to him (as in effect he feels it) that this God of love, satisfied with such few words, reposes again, and rests in the fund and centre of his soul. The experience of these things gives him such an assurance that God is always in the fund or bottom of his soul, that it renders him incapable of doubting it upon any account whatever.

What is your primary doubt about God today? What promise from scripture already refutes that doubt?

Pronounce these words as a declaration over your life: "I am content and satisfied in God. I will enjoy the treasure He is to me. I will not be worried, searching after God's heart. God's heart is open to me; I may dwell in Him and He in me."

Judge by this what content and satisfaction he enjoys while he continually finds in himself so great a treasure. He is no longer in an anxious search after it, but has it open before him, and may take what he pleases of it.

Where might your doubt and unbelief—possibly your busyness—be hindering the current of grace God wants to lavish upon you?

He complains much of our blindness, and cries often that we are to be pitied who content ourselves with so little. *God,* saith he, *has infinite treasure to bestow, and we take up with a little sensible devotion, which passes in a moment. Blind as we are, we hinder God, and stop the current of His graces.*

But when He finds a soul penetrated with a lively faith, He pours into it His graces and favors plentifully: there they flow like a torrent, which, after being forcibly stopped against its ordinary course, when it has found a passage, spreads itself with impetuosity and abundance.

When was the last time you poured the love of God "with impetuosity and abundance" upon another person? Let that be your pursuit this day!

If today was the last day of your life, how would it be spent? How would it be spent if the love of God was all you had to offer others?

Yes, we often stop this torrent by the little value we set upon it. But let us stop it no more; let us enter into ourselves and break down the bank which hinders it. Let us make way for grace; let us redeem the lost time, for perhaps we have but little left.

Death follows us close; let us be well prepared for it: for we die but once; and a miscarriage *there* is irretrievable.

Do you fear death? Why or why not?

I say again, let us enter into ourselves. The time presses, there is no room for delay: our souls are at stake. I believe you have taken such effectual measures that you will not be surprised. I commend you for it; it is the one thing necessary.

When you are alone and silent, what do you most immediately think upon? Do you wish your first recourse was in other directions?

Jesus said that "the Father gives the Holy Spirit to those who ask Him" (Lk. 11:13). Ask today for a greater experience of the presence of the Holy Spirit.

We must, nevertheless, always work at it, because not to advance in the spiritual life is to go back. But those who have the gale of the Holy Spirit go forward even in sleep.

What "storm" in your life needs calming today?

If the vessel of our soul is still tossed with winds and storms, let us awake the Lord, who reposes in it, and He will quickly calm the sea.

Are you "inflamed" or "cooled" in your affections for God today? Talk to Him about your answer.

I have taken the liberty to impart to you these good sentiments, that you may compare them with your own. It will serve again to kindle and inflame them, if by misfortune (which God forbid, for it would be indeed a great misfortune) they should be, though never so little, cooled.

List the qualities of your "first fervor" in the Lord. Which of those do you want to recapture?

Spend time in prayer for specific brothers and sisters today. Let them know you have been praying for them.

Let us then *both* recall our first fervors. Let us profit by the example and the sentiments of this brother, who is little known of the world, but known of God, and extremely caressed by Him.

I will pray for you; do you pray instantly for me....

Fifth Letter

I RECEIVED THIS DAY two books and a letter from Sister ——, who is preparing to make her profession, and upon that account desires the prayers of your holy society, and yours in particular. I perceive that she reckons much upon them; pray do not disappoint her. Beg of God that she may make her sacrifice in the view of His love alone, and with a firm resolution to be wholly devoted to Him. I will send you one of these books which treat of *the presence of God*; a subject which, in my opinion, contains the whole spiritual life; and it seems to me that whoever duly practices it will soon become spiritual.

I know that for the right practice of it, the heart must be empty of all other things; because God will possess the heart *alone*; and as He cannot possess it *alone* without emptying it of all besides, so neither can He act *there*, and do in it what He pleases, unless it be left vacant to Him.

There is not in the world a kind of life more sweet and delightful than that of a continual conversation with God. Those only can comprehend it who practice and experience it; yet I do not advise you to do it from that motive. It is not pleasure which we ought to seek in this exercise; but let us do it from a principle of love, and because God would have us.

Were I a preacher, I should, above all other things, preach the practice of *the presence of* God; and, were I a director, I should advise all the world to do it, so necessary do I think it, and so easy too.

Ah! knew we but the want we have of the grace and assistance of God, we should never lose sight of Him, no, not for a moment. Believe me; make immediately a holy and firm resolution never more wilfully to forget Him,

and to spend the rest of your days in His sacred presence, deprived for the love of Him, if He thinks fit, of all consolations.

Set heartily about this work, and if you do it as you ought, be assured that you will soon find the effects of it. I will assist you with my prayers, poor as they are. I recommend myself earnestly to yours and those of your holy society being theirs, and more particularly

Yours, &c.

Who is someone you know who is entering into a new, important commitment or stage in their life? Pray specifically for them—and let them know.

I received this day two books and a letter from Sister ——, who is preparing to make her profession, and upon that account desires the prayers of your holy society, and yours in particular. I perceive that she reckons much upon them; pray do not disappoint her. Beg of God that she may make her sacrifice in the view of His love alone, and with a firm resolution to be wholly devoted to Him.

I will send you one of these books which treat of *the presence of God*; a subject which, in my opinion, contains the whole spiritual life; and it seems to me that whoever duly practices it will soon become spiritual.

Ask a godly friend for a book recommendation that will draw your heart to God. Procure that book. Begin it as soon as possible.

I know that for the right practice of it, the heart must be empty of all other things; because God will possess the heart *alone*; and as He cannot possess it *alone* without emptying it of all besides, so neither can He act *there*, and do in it what He pleases, unless it be left vacant to Him.

What needs to vacate your heart and its affections?

Create a new, simple, repeatable prayer that you can enjoy with God for this particular day. Keep it in heart and mind all day by affectionate repetition.

There is not in the world a kind of life more sweet and delightful than that of a continual conversation with God. Those only can comprehend it who practice and experience it; yet I do not advise you to do it from that motive.

Throughout the day, renew your vows of love to God. Tell Him. Tell Him constantly.

It is not pleasure which we ought to seek in this exercise; but let us do it from a principle of love, and because God would have us.

Were I a preacher, I should, above all other things, preach the practice of *the presence of God*; and, were I a director, I should advise all the world to do it, so necessary do I think it, and so easy too.

Tell someone about the experience you've been having following in Brother Lawrence's footsteps. Invite them into the joy of their own deeper journey with Jesus.

Ah! knew we but the want we have of the grace and assistance of God, we should never lose sight of Him, no, not for a moment. Believe me; make immediately a holy and firm resolution never more wilfully to forget Him, and to spend the rest of your days in His sacred presence, deprived for the love of Him, if He thinks fit, of all consolations.

What sight or sound reminds you most of the goodness and nearness of God? What focuses your attentions the most quickly in His direction?

What is one concrete "takeaway" you've already received from this journey with Brother Lawrence?

Set heartily about this work, and if you do it as you ought, be assured that you will soon find the effects of it.

Make time today to pray with a beloved brother or sister in Christ.

I will assist you with my prayers, poor as they are.

Sixth Letter

To the Same.

I have received from Mrs. ——, the things which you gave her for me. I wonder that you have not given me your thoughts of the little book I sent to you, and which you must have received. Pray set heartily about the practice of it in your old age: it is better late than never.

I cannot imagine how religious persons can live satisfied without the practice of *the presence of God*. For my part. I keep myself retired with Him in the fund or centre of my soul as much as I can; and while I am so with Him I fear nothing, but the least turning from Him is insupportable.

This exercise does not much fatigue the body; it is, however, proper to deprive it sometimes, nay often; of many little pleasures which are innocent and lawful, for God will not permit that a soul which desires to be devoted entirely to Him should take other pleasures than with Him: that is more than reasonable.

I do not say that therefore we must put any violent constraint upon ourselves. No, we must serve God in a holy freedom; we must do our business faithfully; without trouble or disquiet, recalling our mind to God mildly, and with tranquility, as often as we find it wandering from Him.

It is, however, necessary to put our whole trust in God, laying aside all other cares, and even some particular forms of devotion, though very good in themselves, yet such as one often engages in unreasonably, because these devotions are only means to attain to the end. So when by this exercise of *the presence of* God we are *with Him* who is our end, it is then useless to return to the means;

but we may continue with Him our commerce of love, persevering in His holy presence, one while by an act of praise, of adoration or of desire; one while by an act of resignation or thanksgiving; and in all the ways which our spirit can invent.

Be not discouraged by the repugnance which you may find in it from nature; you must do yourself violence. At the first one often thinks it lost time, but you must go on, and resolve to persevere in it to death, notwithstanding all the difficulties that may occur. I recommend myself to the prayers of your holy society, and yours in particular. I am, in our Lord,

Yours, &c.

Today, reach out to a brother or sister who you seldom talk to and catch up. Make the point of your contact to be an encouragement to his/her spirit.

Do something today that you've been putting off. Do it joyfully in the living presence of God.

I have received from Mrs. ——, the things which you gave her for me. I wonder that you have not given me your thoughts of the little book I sent to you, and which you must have received.

Pray set heartily about the practice of it in your old age: it is better late than never.

I cannot imagine how religious persons can live satisfied without the practice of *the presence of God*. For my part. I keep myself retired with Him in the fund or centre of my soul as much as I can; and while I am so with Him I fear nothing, but the least turning from Him is insupportable.

This exercise does not much fatigue the body; it is, however, proper to deprive it sometimes, nay often; of many little pleasures which are innocent and lawful, for God will not permit that a soul which desires to be devoted entirely to Him should take other pleasures than with Him: that is more than reasonable.

"Retire" with God today—whatever that might mean to you and Him. Enjoy simply being together.

Plan a day of fasting—from sundown to sundown—for the very near future. Commune with God all day that day. Tell no one else.

Conduct today's business with a faithful, mild, tranquil spirit. Enjoy the freedom you have and carry yourself like a truly free person.

List out today's particular worries. Pray through them—and release them back to God.

I do not say that therefore we must put any violent constraint upon ourselves. No, we must serve God in a holy freedom; we must do our business faithfully; without trouble or disquiet, recalling our mind to God mildly, and with tranquility, as often as we find it wandering from Him.

It is, however, necessary to put our whole trust in God, laying aside all other cares, and even some particular forms of devotion, though very good in themselves, yet such as one often engages in unreasonably, because these devotions are only means to attain to the end.

So when by this exercise of *the presence of God* we are *with Him* who is our end, it is then useless to return to the means; but we may continue with Him our commerce of love, persevering in His holy presence, one while by an act of praise, of adoration or of desire; one while by an act of resignation or thanksgiving; and in all the ways which our spirit can invent.

By whatever means necessary, move into nearer experience of the presence of God this day. And endeavor to stay there!

Listen for the voice of the Lord today. Is there something specific He is asking of you?

Be not discouraged by the repugnance which you may find in it from nature; you must do yourself violence. At the first one often thinks it lost time, but you must go on, and resolve to persevere in it to death, notwithstanding all the difficulties that may occur.

"We have but little TIME TO LIVE... Let us LIVE and DIE with GOD"

Seventh Letter

I PITY YOU MUCH. It will be of great importance if you can leave the care of your affairs to ——, and spend the remainder of your life only in worshipping God. He requires no great matters of us; a little remembrance of Him from time to time; a little adoration; sometimes to pray for His grace, sometimes to offer Him your sufferings, and sometimes to return Him thanks for the favors He has given you, and still gives you, in the midst of your troubles, and to console yourself with Him the oftenest you can. Lift up your heart to Him, sometimes even at your meals, and when you are in company: the least little remembrance will always be acceptable to Him. You need not cry very loud; He is nearer to us than we are aware of.

It is not necessary for being with God to be always at church: we may make an oratory of our heart wherein to retire from time to time to converse with Him in meekness, humility and love. Every one is capable of such familiar conversation with God, some more, some less: He knows what we can do. Let us begin, then. Perhaps He expects but one generous resolution on our part. Have courage. We have but little time to live; you are near sixty-four, and I am almost eighty. Let us live and die with God. Sufferings will be sweet and pleasant to us while we are with Him; and the greatest pleasures will be, without Him, a cruel punishment to us. May He be blessed for all. Amen.

Accustom yourself, then, by degrees thus to worship Him, to beg His grace, to offer Him your heart from time to time in the midst of your business, even every moment, if you can. Do not always scrupulously confine yourself to certain rules, or particular forms of devotion, but act with a general confidence in

God, with love and humility. You may assure —— of my poor prayers, and that I am their servant, and particularly

    Yours in our Lord, &c.

What is one needless worry that is consuming your thoughts?
Might it be time to let it go?—and actively move on?

I pity you much. It will be of great importance if you can leave the care of your affairs to ——, and spend the remainder of your life only in worshipping God.

He requires no great matters of us; a little remembrance of Him from time to time; a little adoration; sometimes to pray for His grace, sometimes to offer Him your sufferings, and sometimes to return Him thanks for the favors He has given you, and still gives you, in the midst of your troubles, and to console yourself with Him the oftenest you can.

Which of the actions listed in this reading most felt like they were "for you"? Why so?

Use your mealtime prayers all day to re-center your heart upon the presence of God.

Lift up your heart to Him, sometimes even at your meals, and when you are in company: the least little remembrance will always be acceptable to Him.

All day today, whisper the words, "You are with me right now," as a prayer and reminder of His proximity.

You need not cry very loud; He is nearer to us than we are aware of.

It is not necessary for being with God to be always at church: we may make an oratory of our heart wherein to retire from time to time to converse with Him in meekness, humility and love. Every one is capable of such familiar conversation with God, some more, some less: He knows what we can do. Let us begin, then.

Take another walk with Him and simply enjoy the sights, sounds, smells around you: let Him draw your heart to what draws His heart.

Perhaps He expects but one generous resolution on our part.

Do one generous thing today.

What in your life is calling you to greater courage? Ask God for additional courage and take heart! He is with you!

Have courage.

Write out the eulogy for yourself that you would hope is your life's legacy. Then, today, live so as to make it so.

We have but little time to live; you are near sixty-four, and I am almost eighty. Let us live and die with God.

What is something that presently feels like a suffering for you? How might God be attempting to meet you in that place?

Sufferings will be sweet and pleasant to us while we are with Him; and the greatest pleasures will be, without Him, a cruel punishment to us. May He be blessed for all. Amen.

Write out a list of all the things you're confident about in God. Dig deep. Name as many as possible.

Accustom yourself, then, by degrees thus to worship Him, to beg His grace, to offer Him your heart from time to time in the midst of your business, even every moment, if you can. Do not always scrupulously confine yourself to certain rules, or particular forms of devotion, but act with a general confidence in God, with love and humility.

Eighth Letter
Concerning wandering thoughts in Prayer

YOU TELL ME nothing new; you are not the only one that is troubled with wandering thoughts. Our mind is extremely roving; but, as the will is mistress of all our faculties, she must recall them, and carry them to God as their last end.

When the mind, for want of being sufficiently reduced by recollection at our first engaging in devotion, has contracted certain bad habits of wandering and dissipation, they are difficult to overcome, and commonly draw us, even against our wills, to the things of the earth.

I believe one remedy for this is to confess our faults, and to humble ourselves before God. I do not advise you to use multiplicity of words in prayer: many words and long discourses being often the occasions of wandering. Hold yourself in prayer before God, like a dumb or paralytic beggar at a rich man's gate. Let it be *your* business to keep your mind in the presence of the Lord. If it sometimes wanders and withdraws itself from Him, do not much disquiet yourself for that: trouble and disquiet serve rather to distract the mind than to re-collect it: the will must bring it back in tranquility. If you persevere in this manner, God will have pity on you.

One way to re-collect the mind easily in the time of prayer, and preserve it more in tranquility, is *not to let it wander too far at other times*: you should keep it strictly in the presence of God; and being accustomed to think of Him often, you will find it easy to keep your mind calm in the time of prayer, or at least to recall it from its wanderings.

I have told you already at large, in my former letters, of the advantages we may draw from this practice of the presence of God: let us set about it seriously, and pray for one another.

Yours, &c.

What is the subject of your mind's most active "roving"? Why?

Spend time in prayer asking for a greater draw to the things of Heaven; a lesser pull unto "the things of the earth."

You tell me nothing new; you are not the only one that is troubled with wandering thoughts. Our mind is extremely roving; but, as the will is mistress of all our faculties, she must recall them, and carry them to God as their last end.

When the mind, for want of being sufficiently reduced by recollection at our first engaging in devotion, has contracted certain bad habits of wandering and dissipation, they are difficult to overcome, and commonly draw us, even against our wills, to the things of the earth.

I believe one remedy for this is to confess our faults, and to humble ourselves before God.

What is your greatest point of personal pride? Talk about that with the God who made you.

I do not advise you to use multiplicity of words in prayer: many words and long discourses being often the occasions of wandering. Hold yourself in prayer before God, like a dumb or paralytic beggar at a rich man's gate. Let it be *your* business to keep your mind in the presence of the Lord.

Pray "the Lord's prayer" only today. Let it be the simple prayer of your attentive heart.

Spend today not "beating yourself up" about the wandering nature of your mind. Note it—and then, in tranquility, offer it up to God again instead.

What is the present cause of most of your mind's wandering? Write a prayer, offering it unreservedly to God's care.

If [your mind] sometimes wanders and withdraws itself from Him, do not much disquiet yourself for that: trouble and disquiet serve rather to distract the mind than to re-collect it: the will must bring it back in tranquility. If you persevere in this manner, God will have pity on you.

One way to re-collect the mind easily in the time of prayer, and preserve it more in tranquility, is *not to let it wander too far at other times*: you should keep it strictly in the presence of God; and being accustomed to think of Him often, you will find it easy to keep your mind calm in the time of prayer, or at least to recall it from its wanderings.

I have told you already at large, in my former letters, of the advantages we may draw from this practice of the presence of God: let us set about it seriously, and pray for one another.

Ask God to reveal to you a brother or sister who He knows especially needs your prayer today. Then pray for them throughout this day. Tonight, let them know.

Ninth Letter

THE ENCLOSED IS AN ANSWER to that which I received from ——; pray deliver it to her. She seems to me full of good will, but she would go faster than grace. One does not become holy all at once. I recommend her to you: we ought to help one another by our advice, and yet more by our good examples. You will oblige me to let me hear of her from time to time, and whether she be very fervent and very obedient.

Let us thus think often that our only business in this life is to please God, and that all besides is but folly and vanity. You and I have lived about forty years in religion (*i.e.*, a monastic life). Have we employed them in loving and serving God, who by His mercy has called us to this state and for that very end? I am filled with shame and confusion when I reflect on one hand upon the great favors which God has done, and incessantly continues to do me; and on the other, upon the ill use I have made of them, and my small advancement in the way of perfection.

Since by His mercy He gives us still a little time, let us begin in earnest: let us repair the lost time: let us return with a full assurance to that Father of mercies, who is always ready to receive us affectionately. Let us renounce, let us generously renounce, for the love of Him, all that is not Himself; He deserves infinitely more. Let us think of Him perpetually. Let us put all our trust in Him. I doubt not but we shall soon find the effects of it in receiving the abundance of His grace, with which we can do all things, and without which we can do nothing but sin.

We cannot escape the dangers which abound in life without the actual and *continual* help of God: let us then pray to Him for it *continually*. How can

we pray to Him without being with Him? How can we be with Him but in thinking of Him often? And how can we often think of Him, but by a holy habit which we should form of it? You will tell me that I am always saying the same thing. It is true, for this is the best and easiest method I know; and as I use no other, I advise all the world to do it. We must *know* before we can *love*. In order to *know* God, we must often *think* of Him; and when we come to *love* Him, we shall then also think of Him often, for our heart will be with our treasure. This is an argument which well deserves your consideration.

    I am, Yours, &c.

Where, specifically, do you need to give yourself added grace?
Why, specifically, are you hard on yourself in that one area?

The enclosed is an answer to that which I received from ——; pray deliver it to her. She seems to me full of good will, but she would go faster than grace. One does not become holy all at once.

Do you mentor/disciple anyone in the Lord?

I recommend her to you: we ought to help one another by our advice, and yet more by our good examples. You will oblige me to let me hear of her from time to time, and whether she be very fervent and very obedient.

If so, who? What are you currently working to teach them?

If not, why not? Who might be the person you're called to pour God's heart into?

Today's prayer of repetition: "Only to please you, O God!"

Let us thus think often that our only business in this life is to please God, and that all besides is but folly and vanity.

How long have you lived in the love of Jesus? What are the top 3 (or 5 (or 10)) ways you've experienced His mercy in your life with Him?

You and I have lived about forty years in religion (*i.e.*, a monastic life). Have we employed them in loving and serving God, who by His mercy has called us to this state and for that very end?

I am filled with shame and confusion when I reflect on one hand upon the great favors which God has done, and incessantly continues to do me; and on the other, upon the ill use I have made of them, and my small advancement in the way of perfection.

Make it a day of mindfulness of your woefulness before God. And be quick to confess—and to receive His ready mercies!

Since by His mercy He gives us still a little time, let us begin in earnest: let us repair the lost time: let us return with a full assurance to that Father of mercies, who is always ready to receive us affectionately.

Write yourself an affectionate love note from God to you. Let the time spent doing so bring you to a place of full assurance.

By whatever internal means necessary, tear down the wall of distrust between yourself and God today! Ask Him and let Him be who He is to you! Hold nothing back! Accept His love all day long!

Let us renounce, let us generously renounce, for the love of Him, all that is not Himself; He deserves infinitely more. Let us think of Him perpetually. Let us put all our trust in Him. I doubt not but we shall soon find the effects of it in receiving the abundance of His grace, with which we can do all things, and without which we can do nothing but sin.

We cannot escape the dangers which abound in life without the actual and *continual* help of God: let us then pray to Him for it *continually*. How can we pray to Him without being with Him? How can we be with Him but in thinking of Him often? And how can we often think of Him, but by a holy habit which we should form of it?

You will tell me that I am always saying the same thing. It is true, for this is the best and easiest method I know; and as I use no other, I advise all the world to do it.

Close your eyes to pray and conduct the following experiment: Imagine the face of Jesus just on the other side of your closed eyelids, grinning, delighted, ready to hear you. And then pray as you would if He was right there.

For He is.

Flip back through these pages at random. (Let the hand of God be evident even in this "randomness.") Land on a page and repeat its prompts. See what He does this time. Record it below.

Do you think of God? Do you know God? Do you love God? Let your day prove your answers.

We must *know* before we can *love*. In order to *know* God, we must often *think* of Him; and when we come to *love* Him, we shall then also think of Him often, for our heart will be with our treasure. This is an argument which well deserves your consideration.

Tenth Letter

I HAVE HAD A GOOD DEAL of difficulty to bring myself to write to Mr. ——, and I do it now purely because you and Madam —— desire me. Pray write the directions and send it to him. I am very well pleased with the trust which you have in God: I wish that He may increase it in you more and more. We cannot have too much in so good and faithful a Friend, who will never fail us in this world nor in the next.

If Mr. —— makes his advantage of the loss he has had, and puts all his confidence in God, He will soon give him another friend, more powerful and more inclined to serve him. He disposes of hearts as He pleases. Perhaps Mr. —— was too much attached to him he has lost. We ought to love our friends, but without encroaching upon the love due to God, which must be the principal.

Pray remember what I have recommended to you, which is, to think often on God, by day, by night, in your business, and even in your diversions. He is always near you and with you: leave Him not alone. You would think it rude to leave a friend alone who came to visit you: why then must God be neglected? Do not then forget Him, but think on Him often, adore Him continually, live and die with Him; this is the glorious employment of a Christian. In a word, this is our profession; if we do not know it, we must learn it. I will endeavor to help you with my prayers, and am, in our Lord, Yours, &c.

I have had a good deal of difficulty to bring myself to write to Mr. ——, and I do it now purely because you and Madam —— desire me. Pray write the directions and send it to him.

I am very well pleased with the trust which you have in God: I wish that He may increase it in you more and more. We cannot have too much in so good and faithful a Friend, who will never fail us in this world nor in the next.

What is something you've been avoiding doing for the purposes of God? Today, it's time to do it.

List the qualities necessary for being a good friend. How has God, in Jesus, faithfully fulfilled all your listed requirements?

Who is your current earthly best friend? How might you bless their day today—especially in ways unexpected?

If Mr. —— makes his advantage of the loss he has had, and puts all his confidence in God, He will soon give him another friend, more powerful and more inclined to serve him. He disposes of hearts as He pleases.

Are there relationships in your life that hinder your approach to God? What does He want you to do about that?

Perhaps Mr. —— was too much attached to him he has lost. We ought to love our friends, but without encroaching upon the love due to God, which must be the principal.

Ask Him.

Pray remember what I have recommended to you, which is, to think often on God, by day, by night, in your business, and even in your diversions. He is always near you and with you: leave Him not alone. You would think it rude to leave a friend alone who came to visit you: why then must God be neglected?

How would it change your devotional life if you thought of God as "lonely" when you're not with Him? How do you then imagine His face when you do approach?

If your only "job" were to follow God and enjoy Him, how would that change your day-to-day demeanor and outlook at your earthly work? What might your coworkers note about the change? How would your boss?

Do not then forget Him, but think on Him often, adore Him continually, live and die with Him; this is the glorious employment of a Christian. In a word, this is our profession; if we do not know it, we must learn it.

Who should you "help" with your prayers today? Go on—help them!

I will endeavor to help you with my prayers....

Eleventh Letter

I DO NOT PRAY that you may be delivered from your pains, but I pray God earnestly that He would give you strength and patience to bear them as long as He pleases. Comfort yourself with Him who holds you fastened to the cross. He will loose you when He thinks fit. Happy those who suffer with Him: accustom yourself to suffer in that manner, and seek from Him the strength to endure as much, and as long, as He shall judge to be necessary for you. The men of the world do not comprehend these truths, nor is it to be wondered at, since they suffer like what they are, and not like Christians. They consider sickness as a pain to nature, and not as a favor from God; and seeing it only in that light, they find nothing in it but grief and distress. But those who consider sickness as coming from the hand of God, as the effect of His mercy, and the means which He employs for their salvation—such, commonly find in it great sweetness and sensible consolation.

I wish you could convince yourself that God is often (in some sense) nearer to us, and more effectually present with us, in sickness than in health. Rely upon no other Physician; for, according to my apprehension, He reserves your cure to Himself. Put, then, all your trust in Him, and you will soon find the effects of it in your recovery, which we often retard by putting greater confidence in physic than in God.

Whatever remedies you make use of, they will succeed only so far as He permits. When pains come from God, He only can cure them. He often sends diseases of the body to cure those of the soul. Comfort yourself with the sovereign Physician both of the soul and body.

Be satisfied with the condition in which God places you: however happy you may think me, I envy you. Pains and sufferings would be a paradise to me while I should suffer with my God; and the greatest pleasures would be hell to me if I could relish them without Him. All my consolation would be to suffer something for His sake.

I must, in a little time, go to God. What comforts me in this life is, that I now see Him *by faith*; and I see Him in such a manner as might make me say sometimes, *I believe no more, but I see*. I feel what faith teaches us, and in that assurance and that practice of faith, I will live and die with Him.

Continue then always with God: it is the only support and comfort for your affliction. I shall beseech Him to be with you. I present my service.

Yours, &c.

Brother Lawrence gives us a fascinating image here. It makes one think of the thief on the cross next to Jesus who was yet able to glimpse the wonders of His Kingdom...

When you think of being "fastened to the cross" alongside Jesus, how do you see Him? Write or draw the impression that thought makes on you.

I do not pray that you may be delivered from your pains, but I pray God earnestly that He would give you strength and patience to bear them as long as He pleases. Comfort yourself with Him who holds you fastened to the cross. He will loose you when He thinks fit.

Happy those who suffer with Him: accustom yourself to suffer in that manner, and seek from Him the strength to endure as much, and as long, as He shall judge to be necessary for you.

What right now feels like the greatest "suffering" for you? How is God meeting you in it? How would you like Him to meet you in it?

The men of the world do not comprehend these truths, nor is it to be wondered at, since they suffer like what they are, and not like Christians. They consider sickness as a pain to nature, and not as a favor from God; and seeing it only in that light, they find nothing in it but grief and distress.

Reflect on a recent time of personal pain in your life that God used to shape you. Walk back through the steps He took to meet you in that time. How are you "who you are" because of that experience?

In Romans 8, the apostle Paul wrote, "we know that to those who love God, who are called according to his plan, everything that happens fits into a pattern for good." How does this change your day-to-day outlook, even in the midst of trials?

In hardship, how quickly do you tend to go to God? In triumph, how quickly do you tend to go to God? In sickness, how quickly do you tend to go to God? In health, how quickly do you tend to go to God?

But those who consider sickness as coming from the hand of God, as the effect of His mercy, and the means which He employs for their salvation—such, commonly find in it great sweetness and sensible consolation.

I wish you could convince yourself that God is often (in some sense) nearer to us, and more effectually present with us, in sickness than in health. Rely upon no other Physician; for, according to my apprehension, He reserves your cure to Himself.

Put, then, all your trust in Him, and you will soon find the effects of it in your recovery, which we often retard by putting greater confidence in physic than in God.

Go on a walk today and, every few steps, speak aloud these words of declaration: "I trust only You, O God." See how He meets your spirit in affirming your ongoing trust.

Whatever remedies you make use of, they will succeed only so far as He permits. When pains come from God, He only can cure them. He often sends diseases of the body to cure those of the soul. Comfort yourself with the sovereign Physician both of the soul and body.

Is there something in your life that you think is impossible for God to heal or set right? Why do you think that?

Today, regardless of your circumstances, are you "satisfied"? Why or why not?

Be satisfied with the condition in which God places you: however happy you may think me, I envy you. Pains and sufferings would be a paradise to me while I should suffer with my God; and the greatest pleasures would be hell to me if I could relish them without Him. All my consolation would be to suffer something for His sake.

I must, in a little time, go to God. What comforts me in this life is, that I now see Him *by faith*; and I see Him in such a manner as might make me say sometimes, *I believe no more, but I see*.

Write out your known schedule for the day ahead.

If this was to be the last day of your life, how would you live out the elements of that schedule?

If our eventual experience of Heaven were only to be as robust as our living with God TODAY, *what sort of Heaven would it be?*

Ask God to whom you are to present yourself for service today. Then, present yourself to serve them.

I feel what faith teaches us, and in that assurance and that practice of faith, I will live and die with Him.

Continue then always with God: it is the only support and comfort for your affliction. I shall beseech Him to be with you. I present my service.

Twelfth Letter

IF WE WERE WELL accustomed to the exercise of *the presence of* God, all bodily diseases would be much alleviated thereby. God often permits that we should suffer a little to purify our souls and oblige us to continue *with* Him.

Take courage: offer Him your pains incessantly: pray to Him for strength to endure them. Above all, get a habit of entertaining yourself often with God, and forget Him the least you can. Adore Him in your infirmities, offer yourself to Him from time to time, and in the height of your sufferings, beseech Him humbly and affectionately (as a child his father) to make you conformable to His holy-will. I shall endeavor to assist you with my poor prayers.

God has many ways of drawing us to Himself. He sometimes hides Himself from us, but *faith* alone, which will not fail us in time of need, ought to be our support, and the foundation of our confidence, which must be all in God.

I know not how God will dispose of me. I am always happy. All the world suffer; and I, who deserve the severest discipline, feel joys so continual and so great that I can scarce contain them.

I would willingly ask of God a part of your sufferings, but that I know my weakness, which is so great, that if He left me one moment to myself I should be the most wretched man alive. And yet I know not how He can leave me alone, because faith gives me as strong a conviction as sense can do, that He never forsakes us until we have first forsaken Him. Let us fear to leave Him. Let us be always with Him. Let us live and die in His presence. Do you pray for me, as I for you.

I am, Yours, &c.

If we were well accustomed to the exercise of *the presence of God*, all bodily diseases would be much alleviated thereby. God often permits that we should suffer a little to purify our souls and oblige us to continue *with* Him.

What present circumstance that's been personally unenjoyable for you might be a place where God is trying to meet with you?

Take courage: offer Him your pains incessantly: pray to Him for strength to endure them.

Set hourly alarms to go off throughout your day today. At each, stop and pray for courage to trust and obey.

Make a list of ways you'd like to grow in your "entertainment...with God." How is He personally wooing you into a deeper, richer, sweeter walk together?

Spend time in prayer today from this posture:

Imagine you're climbing up into God's lap, nestling into His chest, looking up sweetly with the eyes of a little child trusting His Daddy. Pray like a little, innocent child would pray.

Above all, get a habit of entertaining yourself often with God, and forget Him the least you can.

Adore Him in your infirmities, offer yourself to Him from time to time, and in the height of your sufferings, beseech Him humbly and affectionately (as a child his father) to make you conformable to His holy will.

I shall endeavor to assist you with my poor prayers.

Write out a prayer of blessing for someone you know. Then give it to them.

God has many ways of drawing us to Himself. He sometimes hides Himself from us, but *faith* alone, which will not fail us in time of need, ought to be our support, and the foundation of our confidence, which must be all in God.

How near does God feel to your heart today? Distant and removed? Intimate and right here? Why do you answer that way?

Spend a day "looking for the bright side" of life: happy with the happiness of the favored child of a Great King. Let your joy be your calling card, all day.

I know not how God will dispose of me. I am always happy.

Spend the day attuned to the sufferings of those around you. Lift as many hearts as possible with your joyous, loving outlook. Write tonight of what you experience.

All the world suffer; and I, who deserve the severest discipline, feel joys so continual and so great that I can scarce contain them.

I would willingly ask of God a part of your sufferings, but that I know my weakness, which is so great, that if He left me one moment to myself I should be the most wretched man alive. And yet I know not how He can leave me alone, because faith gives me as strong a conviction as sense can do, that He never forsakes us until we have first forsaken Him.

Call to mind the moment, in your whole life, of your greatest moral failing. Remember how it felt to be living out that moment/season.

God was there—He loved you even then—how does that inform your living of this day?

Pronounce this as your declaration over this day:

"Lord God, I do not want to leave you all day. I want to spend this whole day always with you. May I live and die in the glory of your presence. Amen."

Reach out to a trusted friend and ask them to pray for you about something specific. Ask them, specifically, what you can be praying for them.

Let us fear to leave Him. Let us be always with Him. Let us live and die in His presence.

Do you pray for me, as I for you.

Thirteenth Letter

To the Same.

I am in pain to see you suffer so long. What gives me some ease and sweetens the feelings I have for your griefs is, that they are proofs of God's love towards you. See them in that view and you will bear them more easily. As your case is, it is my opinion that you should leave off human remedies, and resign yourself entirely to the providence of God: perhaps He stays only for that resignation and a perfect trust in Him to cure you. Since, notwithstanding all your cares, physic has hitherto proved unsuccessful, and your malady still increases, it will not be tempting God to abandon yourself in His hands, and expect all from Him.

I told you in my last that He sometimes permits bodily diseases to cure the distempers of the soul. Have courage then: make a virtue of necessity. Ask of God, not deliverance from your pains, but strength to bear resolutely, for the love of Him, all that He should please, and as long as He shall please.

Such prayers, indeed, are a little hard to nature, but most acceptable to God, and sweet to those that love Him. Love sweetens pains; and when one loves God, one suffers for His sake with joy and courage. Do you so, I beseech you: comfort yourself with Him, who is the only Physician of all our maladies. He is the Father of the afflicted, always ready to help us. He loves us infinitely more than we imagine. Love Him, then, and seek no consolation elsewhere. I hope you will soon receive it. Adieu. I will help you with my prayers, poor as they are, and shall always be, in our Lord Yours, &c.

Write down every current way you can see/feel God loving you. Be as detailed as you can possibly be.

I am in pain to see you suffer so long. What gives me some ease and sweetens the feelings I have for your griefs is, that they are proofs of God's love towards you. See them in that view and you will bear them more easily.

Is there a particular place God is inviting you into a more complete surrender? Why do you think that's the place of His invitation?

As your case is, it is my opinion that you should leave off human remedies, and resign yourself entirely to the providence of God: perhaps He stays only for that resignation and a perfect trust in Him to cure you. Since, notwithstanding all your cares, physic has hitherto proved unsuccessful, and your malady still increases, it will not be tempting God to abandon yourself in His hands, and expect all from Him.

What is one concrete act of personal trust in God you can take today? Take that step.

I told you in my last that He sometimes permits bodily diseases to cure the distempers of the soul. Have courage then: make a virtue of necessity.

Reflect on yesterday's step of faith. Write about your experience.

Ask of God, not deliverance from your pains, but strength to bear resolutely, for the love of Him, all that He should please, and as long as He shall please.

Such prayers, indeed, are a little hard to nature, but most acceptable to God, and sweet to those that love Him. Love sweetens pains; and when one loves God, one suffers for His sake with joy and courage.

Pray for a heart of joy for this whole day.
Then, live joyfully—in His presence.

Do you so, I beseech you: comfort yourself with Him, who is the only Physician of all our maladies. He is the Father of the afflicted, always ready to help us. He loves us infinitely more than we imagine.

What does God love about you right now? Make a list.

Is there a "consolation" you've been using as an artificial help lately? Why do you think that is?

Love Him, then, and seek no consolation elsewhere. I hope you will soon receive it. Adieu.

I will help you with my prayers, poor as they are....

Ask someone—IN PERSON—to spend time together in prayer today.

Fourteenth Letter

To the Same.

I render thanks to our Lord for having relieved you a little, according to your desire. I have been often near expiring, but I never was so much satisfied as then. Accordingly, I did not pray for any relief, but I prayed for strength to suffer with courage, humility and love. Ah, how sweet it is to suffer with God! However great the sufferings may be, receive them with love. It is paradise to suffer and be with Him; so that if in this life we would enjoy the peace of paradise we must accustom ourselves to a familiar, humble, affectionate conversation with Him. We must hinder our spirits wandering from Him upon any occasion. We must make our heart a spiritual temple, wherein to adore Him incessantly. We must watch continually over ourselves, that we may not do, nor say, nor think anything that may displease Him. When our minds are thus employed about God, suffering will become full of unction and consolation.

I know that to arrive at this state the beginning is very difficult, for we must act purely in faith. But though it is difficult, we know also that we can do all things with the grace of God, which He never refuses to them who ask it earnestly. Knock, persevere in knocking, and I answer for it that He will open to you in His due time, and grant you all at once what He has deferred during many years. Adieu! Pray to Him for me, as I pray to Him for you. I hope to see Him quickly.

I am, Yours, &c.

I render thanks to our Lord for having relieved you a little, according to your desire. I have been often near expiring, but I never was so much satisfied as then. Accordingly, I did not pray for any relief, but I prayed for strength to suffer with courage, humility and love. Ah, how sweet it is to suffer with God!

Reach back out to the person you prayed with yesterday. Encourage them and send them a word of love and thanks.

However great the sufferings may be, receive them with love. It is paradise to suffer and be with Him; so that if in this life we would enjoy the peace of paradise we must accustom ourselves to a familiar, humble, affectionate conversation with Him.

Set your heart today on living with God as in paradise. Be familiar, humble, affectionate and converse with Him constantly. May it be a day of great joy!

Pray today for a greater inward experience of the Holy Spirit's presence. Sit in silence and wait upon a fresh infilling.

We must hinder our spirits wandering from Him upon any occasion. We must make our heart a spiritual temple, wherein to adore Him incessantly.

Set a timer today and be still before God for 15 minutes. Keep your thoughts stayed on Him alone.

We must watch continually over ourselves, that we may not do, nor say, nor think anything that may displease Him. When our minds are thus employed about God, suffering will become full of unction and consolation.

I know that to arrive at this state the beginning is very difficult, for we must act purely in faith. But though it is difficult, we know also that we can do all things with the grace of God, which He never refuses to them who ask it earnestly.

Where do you feel a present difficulty in your spiritual life? Place that before God today—and see what He does.

Knock, persevere in knocking, and I answer for it that He will open to you in His due time, and grant you all at once what He has deferred during many years. Adieu!

Morning, noon and night today, knock at the door of Heaven.

And wait upon God's answer!

Pray to Him for me, as I pray to Him for you.

As before, reach out to a friend and pray together, for each other, today.

What about Jesus do you most look forward to encountering "in person"? Meditate on that aspect of His personality all day today.

I hope to see Him quickly.

Fifteenth Letter

To the Same.

God knoweth best what is needful for us, and all that He does is for our good. If we knew how much He loves us, we should always be ready to receive equally and with indifference from His Hand the sweet and the bitter: all would please that came from Him. The sorest afflictions never appear intolerable, except when we see them in the wrong light. When we see them as dispensed by the hand of God, when we know that it is our loving Father who abases and distresses us, our sufferings will lose their bitterness, and become even matter of consolation.

Let all our employment be to *know* God: the more one *knows* Him, the more one *desires* to know Him. And as *knowledge* is commonly the measure of *love*, the deeper and more extensive our *knowledge* shall be, the greater will be our *love*: and if our love of God were great, we should love Him equally in pains and pleasures.

Let us not content ourselves with loving God for the mere sensible favors, how elevated soever, which He has done, or may do us. Such favors, though never so great, cannot bring us so near to Him as faith does in one simple act. Let us seek Him often by faith. He is within us: seek Him not elsewhere. If we do love Him alone, are we not rude, and do we not deserve blame, if we busy ourselves about trifles which do not please and perhaps offend Him. It is to be feared these *trifles* will one day cost us dear.

Let us begin to be devoted to Him in good earnest. Let us cast everything besides out of our hearts. He would possess them alone. Beg this favor of Him.

If we do what we can on our parts, we shall soon see that change wrought in us which we aspire after. I cannot thank Him sufficiently for the relaxation He has vouchsafed you. I hope from His mercy the favor to see Him within a few days.[6] Let us pray for one another.

    I am, in our Lord, Yours, &c.

---

6   He took to his bed two days after, and died within the week.

Make a list of things "needful" in your life. How has God already provided each of those things? What does it mean to you that He provides all things WITH LOVE?

God knoweth best what is needful for us, and all that He does is for our good. If we knew how much He loves us, we should always be ready to receive equally and with indifference from His Hand the sweet and the bitter: all would please that came from Him.

The sorest afflictions never appear intolerable, except when we see them in the wrong light. When we see them as dispensed by the hand of God, when we know that it is our loving Father who abases and distresses us, our sufferings will lose their bitterness, and become even matter of consolation.

Is there anything in your life that feels "intolerable" presently? Today, bring that to God's feet and be still before Him. Let Him show you precisely what He is doing with your life.

Today, do whatever will cause an increased experience of your love for God: prayer, worship, reading, thinking, meditating, fasting—it's up to you. Make record of your experience with Him.

Let all our employment be to *know* God: the more one *knows* Him, the more one *desires* to know Him. And as *knowledge* is commonly the measure of *love*, the deeper and more extensive our *knowledge* shall be, the greater will be our *love*: and if our love of God were great, we should love Him equally in pains and pleasures.

Let us not content ourselves with loving God for the mere sensible favors, how elevated soever, which He has done, or may do us. Such favors, though never so great, cannot bring us so near to Him as faith does in one simple act.

Spend today in simple belief in one single promise of God. Let it not leave your heart and mind all day.

Let us seek Him often by faith. He is within us: seek Him not elsewhere.

Go inward, into yourself, and encounter God in your inner life today. Relish His inhabitational proximity!

Are there any "trifles" in your life you're ready to be done with? What has been their history? And why is the Lord God better than them?

Yes, beg this favor today: To be possessed wholly by God; to have a heart fixed on Him alone; to learn the devotion that Jesus had to His Father; to be in good earnest constantly!

If we do love Him alone, are we not rude, and do we not deserve blame, if we busy ourselves about trifles which do not please and perhaps offend Him. It is to be feared these *trifles* will one day cost us dear.

Let us begin to be devoted to Him in good earnest. Let us cast everything besides out of our hearts. He would possess them alone. Beg this favor of Him.

If we do what we can on our parts, we shall soon see that change wrought in us which we aspire after. I cannot thank Him sufficiently for the relaxation He has vouchsafed you. I hope from His mercy the favor to see Him within a few days.[7]

---
[7] He took to his bed two days after, and died within the week.

Let us pray for one another.

What is one particular remembrance from your journey with Brother Lawrence that you'll long remember?

Let us spend today in a state of constant prayer.

About Brother Lawrence

BROTHER LAWRENCE, born Nicolas Herman, was a 17th-century disciple of Jesus whose posthumous *The Practice of the Presence of God* is considered one of the greatest works on intimate union with God ever written. Brother Lawrence lived his entire life in France and, following a short stint as a soldier in the Thirty Years' War, became a lay brother in a Carmelite monastery in Paris. There, for the rest of his life, he attempted to live in abiding connection with God—whether in conversation with others, washing dishes, or making sandals. His testimony, assembled from letters and conversations recorded by friends and admirers, comprises the timeless work *The Practice of the Presence of God*.

About the Illustrator

LIUDMYLA STETSKOVYCH is an illustrator specializing in children's book illustration and working with media art. Lusya currently lives and works in L'viv, Ukraine. After gaining a Master's degree in Graphics and Illustration at the Ukrainian Academy of Printing, she worked as a 2D artist and graphic designer, and eventually devoted herself to illustration. She enjoys engaging her imagination and creativity while working with graphic forms and being inspired by old manuscripts, world art, and native Ukrainian culture.

www.ingramcontent.com/pod-product-compliance
Lightning Source LLC
Chambersburg PA
CBHW081424090426
42740CB00017B/3172